D0878676

Bismillāhir-Rahmānir-Rahīm.
In the name of God,
the Most Compassionate, the Most Merciful.

GOD'S
Psychology

A SUFI EXPLANATION

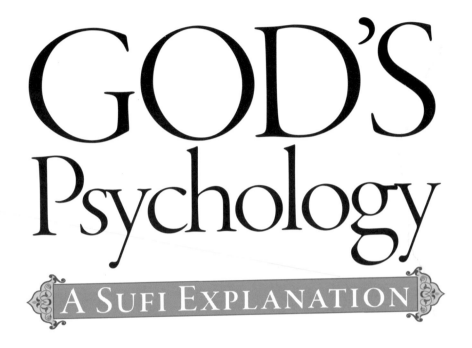

GOD'S
Psychology

A SUFI EXPLANATION

M. R. Bawa Muhaiyaddeen ﭬ

Fellowship Press
Philadelphia, PA

ABOUT THE COVER:

This original "Heart's Work" painting by Muhammad Raheem Bawa Muhaiyaddeen ☉, "The Rocky Mountain of the Heart," was completed on January 28, 1980, and it illustrates the stone-hearted qualities we have grown within ourselves; this mountain is harder than the hardest mountain in creation, and is layered with arrogance, selfishness, religious differences, religious arrogance, conceit, and desire for name, fame, and titles. This hard heart is unmelting and shows no compassion for other lives.

The animals that surround this rocky mountain are representative of the animal qualities that have entered the hearts of mankind. All these animals and even the shrubs and bushes illustrate the distractions that we need to clear from within ourselves. We must then build a place of worship to remember God.

The seven colors in the painting represent the seven states of consciousness within mankind: feeling, awareness, intellect, judgment, wisdom, divine analytic wisdom, and divine luminous wisdom. The fish represent creation, and the swan represents subtle wisdom, the perfection that accepts only purity.

This "Rocky Mountain of the Heart" has to be split open and blasted away, and in its place the house of God's qualities must be built within our own hearts and within our own lives.

(Sources: From a discourse by M. R. Bawa Muhaiyaddeen ☉ given on January 28, 1980 and from *The Tree That Fell to the West: Autobiography of a Sufi*, Chapter Seven, "The Rocky Mountain," December 22, 1983.)

Library of Congress Control Number: 2007923702

Muhaiyaddeen, M. R. Bawa.
    God's psychology: a sufi explanation / M. R. Bawa Muhaiyaddeen.
    Philadelphia, PA: Fellowship Press, 2007
    p. cm.
    Includes index.

Trade paperback	Hardcover
ISBN 13: 978-0-914390-81-7	ISBN 13: 978-0-914390-82-4
ISBN 10: 0-914390-81-3	ISBN 10: 0-914390-82-1

    1. Sufism. 2. Psychology. 3. God. 4. Wisdom. 5. Islam. 6. Religion.
7. Compassion. 8. Purity. 9. Unity. 10. Peace. 11. Understanding.
12. God's Qualities. 13. Love. 14. Truth. I. Title.

Every attempt is made to ensure the accuracy of the translation of these discourses. They are complete and include the entire content of the talks given by Muhammad Raheem Bawa Muhaiyaddeen ☉ on the dates noted at the beginning of the chapters.

Printed in the United States of America by FELLOWSHIP PRESS
Bawa Muhaiyaddeen Fellowship
First Printing

A'ūdhu billāhi minash-shaitānir-rajīm.
I seek refuge in God from the accursed satan.

Bismillāhir-Rahmānir-Rahīm.
In the name of God, the Most Compassionate, the Most Merciful.

ৠ 1 ৡ
Only God Is Not Crazy

March 7, 1982, Sunday 8:05 AM

M*y God help me.*[1] May God help us.
Psychology. *God's psychology.*

Anbu, love. Everything that has appeared in the world since the time it was created is crazy, *pytthiam.*[2] There is nothing that is not crazy. There is no being that is not crazy. Everything is crazy. Every thought is crazy. Every desire is crazy. Every intention is crazy. Every fascination is crazy. Hunger and disease are crazinesses. This birth itself is crazy. Whatever has appeared is crazy. So many tens of millions of crazinesses arise from the five elements—from the particle, from the atom, from the virus, and from the connection of the cells. Anything that attacks another is crazy. Anything that kills another is crazy. Anything that eats another is crazy. Creation is like this.

We must understand that it is God who created this state. There is a Power that transcends *anādi,* the beginningless beginning, and *ādi,* the primal beginning, and goes beyond the beyond,

---

1. Bawa Muhaiyaddeen ☺ often used English words in an unusual way. For the sake of clarity, these words have been italicized.
2. *pytthiam* (T) Craziness, obsession, madness, insanity, derangement, delirium, fixation, compulsion.

and beyond the three (states), *poruls*.[3] That Power manifested this natural creation. Having manifested this creation, that Power alone understands it, and acts accordingly. He (God)[4] alone understands what food should be given to what (creation), how each should be protected, and how each action should be done. He sustains His creations in this way.

He created, for a reason, the trees, grass, weeds, birds, four-legged animals, cells, stones, water, air, ether, fire, sun, moon, stars, the angels, *malaks*, the archangels, *malā'ikat*, the light beings, jinns, fairies, celestial beings, ghosts, demons, satan, earth, sky, everything—creations that move and those that do not move, things that speak and things that do not speak, darkness and light. Like this, God has created these countless creations, these innumerable creations, these endless creations, and He is the only One who understands them and can stop their craziness. He is the only One who is without craziness. Everything else is crazy. There are many tens of millions of crazinesses. Within just one creation there are so many crazinesses.

We must understand Him, that one Treasure that understands all these crazinesses. He is the only One without craziness. He is the One who gives treatment to the soul, *ānmā*. He is the One who treats the *qalb*,[5] inner heart. He is the One who gives comfort, He is the One who gives peace, and He is the One who treats all lives with equality. He is the One who demonstrates

---

3. *porul* (T) Literally means thing, meaning, treasure, reality, truth. Here *poruls* may refer to the three states of *anādi*, the beginningless beginning, *ādi*, the primal beginning, and *awwal*, the time of creation.

4. The editors have placed parentheses around words that are inferred; these words have been added for clarification purposes.

5. *qalb* (A) Heart; the heart within the heart of man; the inner heart. See the Glossary for a further explanation.

equality, tranquility, and peace. That Power makes us find peace and tranquility in the heart.

That Power has no race, no religious fanaticism, no scriptures,
and no philosophies. It is beyond this.
It has no color, no hue, no form, and no shape. It is beyond this.
It has no "I" and no "you." It is beyond this.
It has no night and no day. It is beyond this.
It has no disease, no illness, no hunger, and no old age.
It is beyond this.
It has no pride, no praise, and no differences. It is beyond this.
It has no birth, no death, no end, and no destruction.
It is beyond this.
It has no house, no property, no wife, no children, no relatives,
and no form. It is beyond this.
It has no color, no hue, no language, speech, or breath.
It is beyond this.

That complete Power that always exists and that is beyond
and beyond all this is God.
He has no murder and no sin. He has no desire, no anger,
no miserliness, no attachment, no fanaticism, and no envy.
He has none of these six evils. He is beyond this.
He has no arrogance, no karma, and no maya, illusion.
He is beyond this.
He is beyond the three illusory animal qualities of
tārahan, singhan, and *sūran.*[6]
He has no intoxicants, no lust, no theft, no murder,

---

6. *tārahan, singhan,* and *sūran* (T) The three sons of illusion, related to aspects of the
sexual act.

and no falsehood. He is beyond this.
He is neither male nor female. He is beyond this.

When the *qalb*, inner heart, of any male or female intends Him, that Power comes and gives peace. It is not in a state that can be seen, but functions in a natural way. It is not in a state that can be seen, but with great care causes the creation, man, to reach maturity, and protects him. It is not in a state that can be captured, but is contained naturally within all *qalbs* and warns those *qalbs* about right and wrong. As the conscience, It warns about what is right and what is wrong.

That (Power) has no school, no learning, no teacher, none of these. It takes our wisdom and clarifies it, takes our speech and speaks to us, providing explanations, takes our breath and explains the breath to us, takes our breath and breathes through that, takes our vision and sees through that, takes our conduct and acts through that, takes our wisdom and teaches wisdom to us, takes our vision and gives explanations about what is seen, takes our breath and gives explanations about that breath, takes our speech and gives explanations about the speech, takes wisdom and gives explanations of wisdom, takes the *qalb* and, existing as the *qalb* within the *qalb*, reveals Itself. It looks at our mind and desire, looks at the witness,[7] the wisdom, and the justice, and gives the explanation accordingly.

Existing as Life within life, as the Treasure that does not hurt anyone or anything, It gives life to that life. Taking our hunger, It gives the way to appease that hunger. Taking our sorrows, It ends those sorrows and gives peace through feeling, awareness, and intellect. God is a natural Power like that.

---

7. witness: In Tamil, the word for witness is *chādchi*. The conscience is the witness of the heart.

We cannot analyze this. It cannot be researched. One who sets out to research into God in any way, one who thinks he can finish this study, is a crazy man. He will become crazy. He cannot do it. But the one who touches even one drop of It is a good one, a good one, *nallavar, nallavar.* If he follows with faith and touches one drop or takes one ray, if he takes even one ray from God, that Treasure, and understands it, he will become complete, and his craziness will end. One cannot reach an end to this research. It is God who has to give the explanation.

He conducts Himself with and reveals the five prerequisites of (*Īmān-Islām*)[8]: *porumai,* patience, *sabūr,* inner patience, *shakūr,* contentment, *tawakkul,* surrender, and *al-hamdu lillāh,* giving all praise to Allāh. He exists beyond all this. He has peace and gives that peace to all His creations. He gives qualities through (His) qualities.

Knowing the bad qualities, He gives the good qualities.
Knowing the bad desires, He gives good desires.
Knowing the bad thoughts, He knows and gives good thoughts.
Knowing bad food, He gives good food.
Understanding bad speech, He gives good speech.
Knowing anger, He shows patience.
Knowing injustice, He shows justice.
Knowing thirst, He gives good water.
Knowing the qualities, He acts with good qualities.
Knowing the actions, He displays good actions.
Knowing love, He embraces with good love.

---

8. *Īmān*-Islām (A) See Glossary.

Even if our father and mother forget us, God, who exists in the form of love, will never forget us. He exists in the form of wisdom, in the form of love, in the form of compassion, in the form of patience, in the form of justice, in the form of integrity, and in the form of conscience. He exists in the form that gazes with a compassionate eye. In this way, He exists with the three thousand gracious qualities and the ninety-nine *wilāyats*[9]—His actions and conduct. His qualities are His *wilāyats*, His actions are His *wilāyats*. The Qur'ān speaks of these ninety-nine *wilāyats*. He exists as the One, as the Power. He has given to His creation, man, ninety-nine *wilāyats*, His qualities, actions, and conduct. That Power (God) exists within these and governs everything. Knowing every being, every blade of grass, every weed, tree, bird, cell, worm, virus, snake, scorpion, poisonous being, poison, darkness, light, satan, and ghost, He bestows beneficence without resentment, without anger, without separation, without differences, without the divisiveness of "I" or "you," without lust or enmity, and without attachment, and He guides them. In a beneficent way, He guides and nourishes every being. He exists within beneficial actions, and gives energy, shakti, to all the creatures of the sea, to the creatures on the land, to the birds that fly in the sky, to the reptiles and insects on the earth, to the precious gems buried within the earth, to the stones, trees, sand, mercury, rubies, pure gold, silver, gold, iron, copper, diamonds, tin, and to many tens of millions of chemicals, and through these, He comforts all lives. This is psychology. God's psychology.

God considers each of His creations, all lives from the particle, from the atom, from the cell, from the virus, from things

---

9. *wilāyats* (A) God's Power; that which has been manifested through God's actions; the ninety-nine beautiful names and actions of God.

that are seen to things that are unseen, and He treats them. His treatment:

Knowing every heart, He removes its sorrow.
This is His treatment.
Knowing every *qalb,* He gives treatment.
Knowing the qualities (of all lives), He treats them.
Knowing their actions, He treats them.
Knowing their hunger, He treats them.
Knowing their desire, He treats them.
Knowing their sexual games, *lilai vinotham,* He gives treatment.
He knows their sixty-four arts and sciences, *kalaigal,* and all
their dancing and gives treatment.
He knows their languages and gives treatment.
He knows their speech, their mind, and their qualities
and gives treatment.
He knows their body and treats them.
He knows their blood and treats them.
He knows their air and treats them.
He knows their breath and treats them.
He knows the body made of the five elements of earth, fire,
water, air, and ether and gives treatment.
He knows the mind and desire and gives treatment.
He knows their affection and gives treatment.
He knows their lust and gives treatment.
He knows their lies and gives treatment.
He knows their truth and, existing as Truth to truth,
gives treatment.
He knows their love and gives treatment.
He knows their nature and gives treatment.

governs them. If not for Him, not even an atom would move. He is a Power that exists as Life within all lives. That Power is God. He is the Power that causes everything to move. He dwells within love, within truth, within conscience, within wisdom, *arivu*, within awareness, *unarchi*, within intellect, *putti*, within perception, *unarvu*, within judgment, *madi*, within subtle wisdom, *nup-arivu*, within divine analytic wisdom, *pahut arivu*, within divine luminous wisdom, *pērarivu*, within the divine wisdom of *gnānam*, within the plenitude of His qualities, within His compassion, within His love, within His equality, within His peacefulness, within the gracious qualities of the plenitude of His *Nūr*, the Light, within His judgment, and within His justice.

He is that Justice, He is that Love, He is that Compassion. He does not kill anything. He acts with the Quality within the quality. He acts with the Love within love. He acts with the Goodness within goodness. This is the treatment He gives; this is His medicine. His treatment is the quality that gives peace to all lives. He resplends in the macrocosm and in the microcosm, in the fetus, in the form, in the blood, in water, in air, in earth, in the sky, in the sun, in the moon, in night and in day, in birth and in death, on the inside and the outside, in everything—in the form of love, in the form of justice, and in the form of the witness. As the Witness, He gives the explanation and He warns us.

If a sun can shine its light everywhere without showing differences, then what kind of Power and in what kind of state is the One who created this sun? We must understand this. Man must realize this. We must understand what kind of Power created this sun. With firm certitude and faith, we must accept this Power (God) and His qualities. One who is a human being, *mānidan*,[11]

---

11. *mānidan* (T) Man, human being. Depending on the context, *mānidan* may refer either to a realized human being or to mankind in general.

and all the animals have accepted this Power.

God provides food and protection to the blade of grass. He gives water and protection to the tree. He gives different qualities and many different shaktis, energies, to the weeds and protects them. He gives many different fragrances to the weeds and the flowers and protects them. He has created each of them differently. He has given them particular qualities, medicinal properties, fragrances, poisons, beneficial or harmful effects, and tastes. Each flower and each seed has been given various qualities. Each leaf has been given various qualities. All of these are His treatment, and He dispenses this treatment everywhere. He has placed His qualities within everything and nurtures each (thing) in the section of goodness.

To cut the section of evil, to cut darkness, He has spread light everywhere. To cut evil, He has placed goodness. To cut bad qualities, He has placed the good qualities, and then protects them. To dispel desire, He has placed the good qualities of God. To cut the karma of birth, He has placed love, wisdom, and truth. To cut arrogance, He has placed wisdom. To cut karma, He has placed the good qualities of wisdom. To cut maya, illusion, He has placed that Power, that Justice called God. To cut falsehood, He has given truth. To cut evil qualities, He has given good qualities. To dispel anger, He has given patience. To dispel pride, He has given humility. To dispel hunger, He has placed *sabūr,* inner patience, and *shakūr,* contentment.

Since both good and evil are intermingled in every tree, every weed, every blade of grass, in water, in all created things, there is a section of craziness that also exists in them. Everything that has been created with the five elements has craziness. All lives are crazy. Except for Him, except for that Power, everything is crazy. Good and bad are both crazy. Good qualities and bad qualities are both crazy. If they (the creations) do not understand, they are crazy. They have love and hate. That is crazy. They have faith and lack of faith, ignorance. That is crazy. They have truth and falsehood, they have the "I" and the "we." That is crazy. This exists in every action. There is the selfishness of "my hunger" and also the awareness and compassion of the need to appease the hunger of others.

Like this, in God's research, His treatment is to cure these craziness with the good section of His love, compassion, justice, integrity, good conduct, embracing everyone with His conscience, mercy, patience, peacefulness, and selfless duty. Without keeping anything for Himself, He protects and embraces all lives from the earth to the sky, from the atom to the virus, from the six kinds of lives to the Light, from birth to death, and from the questioning to the judgment.[12] He understands and helps every being. That is His treatment. He does this without anger, without sin, without selfishness, without differences, without race, without religion, without separation, without wrath, without craziness, without desire, without lust, without malice, without hastiness, without impatience, without the "I," and without the "you." God does this duty with His three thousand gracious qualities, His ninety-nine qualities, His actions, conduct, and justice. That Treasure is the One who provides treatment. This is His psychology treatment.

He has the connection of heart to heart, the connection of wisdom to wisdom, the connection of truth to truth, the connection of life to life, and the connection of good to good. Like this, He has the connection to the four qualities of modesty, re-

---

12. questioning to judgment: After a human being is buried, he or she is questioned in the grave by the Angels Munkar ☻ and Nakīr ☻. Judgment is given by God.

serve, shyness, and fear of wrongdoing. He has the connection to good conduct, the connection to good thoughts, the connection to good intentions, the connection to good actions, the connection to love, the connection to giving comfort, and the connection to compassion. Like this, He is the One who has this kind of connection to everything, and with this connection, He is the One who cures the sins and crazinesses. He is the *Good* Physician Psychologist.

He is the Physician for wisdom, the Physician for *gnānam,* divine wisdom, the Physician for the soul, the Physician for the body, the Physician for the *qalb,* inner heart, the Physician for the vision, the Physician for the mind, and the Physician for the thoughts.

To remove poison, He has given power to certain weeds.
He has given fragrance to the flower so it will be enjoyed.
He has given scent to the tree so it will be loved.
He has given love to the seed to appease the hunger of everyone.
He has given awareness to the grass so it can feed and appease
the hunger of others.
He has given taste to water so it can quench the thirst of all.
To another section of water, the ocean water, He has given the
taste of salt and reveals the salty taste in food.
In each thing He displays an opposite.

Like this, to every creation He shows the taste and, through this, makes their *qalbs* peaceful. In His love and His compassion, without beating, without speaking, without striking, without murdering, and without punishing, He understands the mind and gives treatment. He understands the actions and gives treatment.

He understands the behavior and gives treatment. He knows the vision and gives treatment. He looks at the face, observing if it is tired, and gives treatment. He observes if the body is healthy or if the *qalb* is suffering or if there is a lack of blood. He finds out what is lacking and then treats it. This is what He does, this is His treatment.

Like this, He is the Physician who knows, He is the Physician who understands everything, the Physician of love, the Physician of compassion, the Physician of wisdom, the Physician of justice, the Physician of truth, the Physician without selfishness, the One who gives peace—Āndavan, God, Allāh. He is a Power. That Power has no form or shape. It dwells in all lives, in the weeds and in the grass, dwelling here and there, everywhere and in everything. It is within everything, on the inside and the outside, in day and in night, in sleep and in wakefulness, in speech and in breath. That Power is spread everywhere, watching and treating everyone. That Treasure is all-pervasive, outspread everywhere.

We who are human beings must realize the kind of treatment God is giving. Then we will understand that this treatment is psychology. He knows, He understands, and then gives treatment. What treatment does He give? Is it medicine? His medicine is love. Does He use sticks or needles or electric current? No. His medicine is compassion, patience, love, forbearance, tolerance, dedication to others, justice—losing Himself and embracing everyone with love, breast to breast, love to love, life to life, good conduct to good conduct. He selflessly embraces heart to heart, good qualities to good qualities.

He cuts the bad qualities and gives the good. He cuts bad illness and gives good health. He cuts bad thoughts and gives good thoughts. He cuts bad desires and gives what is good. He cuts sinful lust and gives what is good. He cuts bad attachments and gives what is good. He cuts bad actions and gives good ones. He cuts jealousy and gives patience. He cuts doubt and gives peace. He cuts selfishness and gives *sabūr*, inner patience. He cuts differences and gives unity.

Like this, man must reflect upon the qualities God gives, the way He cures these diseases, and the way He gives peace. A man with wisdom must think of this. This is the psychology treatment God gives with understanding. If I were to go on talking only about His treatment, if I were to go on speaking only about His ways of treatment, His qualities, and His justice, it would take a trillion years to tell only one portion of it. I would need a trillion years to speak about His ways of treatment. What I have spoken about now amounts to only an atom's worth. The One who has these qualities is called God—this Power.

If someone wants to become a healer, a doctor, a psychologist, or a human being, if someone wants to do any of these duties, for such a one He (God) is the Guru. He is the Father, He is the Brother, He is the Grandfather, He is the Great-Grandfather, He is God. He is the Mother and the Father. He takes on all these different roles and plays with us. He is the Baby who plays with us, He is the small One, He is the One who embraces us, He is the One who calls us, He is the One who loves us. This One who assumes these tens of millions of different roles and thoughts is called the Grandfather and the Father, and we must embrace Him. We must imbibe His love. We must intermingle in His heart and in His love.

First we must change into a human being. Once we become a human being, we can know the qualities of our Father, His actions, behavior, good conduct, and the way He does His duty. We can know about those qualities. We can learn those ways. We must follow our Grandfather, our Father, and have faith in Him.

To have faith in that Power is to have faith in God.

One who does not have this faith can never become a human being, and if he does not become a human being, he will never realize *pahut arivu,* divine analytic wisdom, or love. He will only know about killing lives and eating them. He will only know about ganja, opium, marijuana, murder, drugs, LSD, alcohol, and lust. He will only know about what the animals do, and he will act the way they act. Animals defecate where they eat and sleep where they defecate. This is the way a man will act if he is in this state.

First and foremost, man needs our God, the Father. That is the Guru. That is God. That is the just God, the compassionate God, the loving God, the God who protects us, embraces us, and shows us the way. If we want to give treatment, we must believe in Him and learn from Him. We must join with That (Him) and learn from That. We must enter That and learn from That. We must enter those qualities, learn those qualities, and then give treatment. We must go within those actions and then give treatment.

One must first treat himself. He must become a human being and treat himself. This is not written in books or in all the tens of millions of (kinds of) research. Those researches are a different section; they exhibit the world and the qualities of the world. They show the love, the qualities, and the actions of the world.

What will a monkey do? It will do what it sees. Can it do anything beyond this? No, it cannot. It mimics whatever it sees. It cannot think or do anything for itself. If someone eats, it will eat. If someone wearing a hat puts it down, the monkey will pick it up and put it on its head. If someone throws something, the monkey will throw something. If someone smiles, the monkey will smile. If someone urinates while standing, the monkey will urinate while standing. It mimics whatever others do.

This is the way of the learning of the world, to mimic what others do, to do what illusion does. The mind, the monkey mind, is like this, it will mimic whatever it sees. It will look at what the world is doing and imitate it. Love, sex, the sexual games, taking LSD and drugs—it will mimic these.

Everything the world displays is the learning that belongs to the left side, to the section of the world. This is not the learning of the right side. We must cut away the learning of the left side; we must cut away hunger, sex, and the sexual games. The learning that can dispel these is the learning of God, our Father. If we have love for Him, if we go towards Him, if we have faith and determination, and if that Power speaks with us, then we can learn about (giving) treatment. We can become a human being, and if we do, we can obtain the qualities from this Power.

This is inside, this learning is within. When you learn one thing, you cut away another thing; you cut away something that is killing you. When you learn something else, you cut away your sin. When you learn something else, you cut away your karma. When you learn something else, you cut away your illusion. When you learn something else, you cut away your ignorance. When you learn something else, you cut away your anger. When you learn something else, you cut away your evil. When you learn something else, you cut away your differences. When you learn something else, you cut away your selfishness. When you learn something else, you cut away your blood ties. When you learn something else, you cut away your falsehood. When you learn something else, you cut away your birth. When you learn something else, you cut away your attachments and your bad qualities. When you learn something else, you cut away your thoughts.

Like this, you will learn to cut the countless thoughts—the *nānūr lacham kōdi ten thousand*, four hundred trillion, ten thousand demonic (thoughts)—and the one hundred and five million animal births.

Having cut these, you will acquire your Father's qualities of compassion, patience, justice, integrity, peacefulness, giving comfort, duty, actions, *sabūr*, inner patience, *shakūr*, contentment, *tawakkul*, surrender, and *al-hamdu lillāh*, His praise. You will surrender to your Father.

When you surrender yourself to that Power,
then what can you do?
When you have surrendered in this way,
you can become a physician.
What will your treatment be? His qualities.
What love will you have? His love with which you embrace.
What medicine will you use? His compassion.
What is His justice? Your conscience that is without differences.
What is His integrity? Truth.
What is He? The Truth, the Plenitude, the Power,
the Complete Power.
What is God? Your soul.

God is the Soul within your soul—the Soul within the soul,
the Life within the life,
the Soul-Life, the *Ānmā-Uyir.*

When you understand this, what will the lives of others be?
Your life.
What will the hunger of others be? Your hunger.
What will the sorrow of others be? Your sorrow.
What will the justice of others be? Your justice.

The lives of others will be your life; the suffering of others will be your suffering. Wherever something happens, it will be as if it happened to you. Wherever there is destruction, it will be your destruction. Whenever someone sins, it will be your sin. Whenever someone experiences hunger, disease, old age, and death, it will be yours. You must understand this.

As soon as a mosquito bites, you brush it away, do you not? In the same way, when you become a human being and when the sorrows of others come to bite you, you can immediately brush them away, *oh, oh, oh, oh.* When something crawls on your body, you immediately brush it away, do you not? Since all lives are born with you and are a part of your body, therefore, if sorrow comes to anyone, you can brush it away just as you brush away an insect from your body. Since all lives are contained within your *qalb*, your eyes, your mind, your entire body, if anything happens to another, it can be brushed away.

Your faults are the disease, and that is craziness. There is truth and falsehood. There are the ways of the five kinds of lives. And there is the soul, God's Power, and that is one of the six kinds of lives. That is one Point; the others have many points. The many points are the world; the one Point is God, Truth. Until you come to this one Point, you are crazy. Once you reach this one Point, you are the physician, the physician of compassion and love, and then you can give treatment. Then you become the psychologist, the doctor. Then you will not look for medicine for the patient. First, your *qalb* should go and connect with the *qalb* of the patient. Your love should go and connect to that love, your smile should go and connect to that smile, your water should go and put out that fire, your compassion should go and cure the suffering, your good qualities should go and change the bitterness within him that prevents him from drinking, and your honey should go and change the water of birth.

In this way, the countless thoughts of God should go and change the thoughts and embrace the heart. Do not embrace the body, embrace the heart. The heart should embrace the heart. If you embrace the heart, the illness will leave. You will not need any medicine. If you can first treat the heart, then giving medicine (later) is easy. The medicine will work later. But if you do not treat the heart, the medicine will not work.

If you add milk to boiling water, the milk will not settle; it will splatter from the pot. First you must still the water before pouring in the milk. Then it will remain in the pot. If you plant a seed while the earth is moving, the seed will be swallowed by the earth. But if you first level the earth and then plant the seed, it will stay where you plant it, and will grow and give benefit. The benefit of medicine is like this, the benefit of wisdom is like this, the benefit of good qualities is like this, and the benefit of curing illness is like this. First you must comfort a person and then treat him. First you must become a doctor, a psychologist, and a human being. This learning is learned on the inside. We must think of this.

My love you.[13] Please think of this. Man, the son,[14] must take on the qualities of his Father, act with those qualities, and give treatment with those qualities. If you do not have that state, everything else that you have learned will be just like the work a monkey does. All the other learning will be monkey work, but if you have realized *this* learning and do the work of a man, then your treatment will be the treatment of love.

---

13. My love you: This phrase is often used by Bawa Muhaiyaddeen ☻. He said that the use of "I" was inappropriate when referring to God's love.

14. Man, the son: A child of God who has perfected himself or herself through grace and who has merged with the Light of God.

Please think a little about the learning a human being should learn. The treatment given by a human being is psychology. Think about that psychology. The whole world is crazy. The world is crazy, everything that has been created is crazy. We will talk about this craziness later.

A'ūdhu billāhi minash-shaitānir-rajīm.
I seek refuge in God from the accursed satan.

Bismillāhir-Rahmānir-Rahīm.
In the name of God, the Most Compassionate, the Most Merciful.

God's Love Can Cure All Craziness

March 7, 1982, Sunday 9:40 AM

With faith and certitude, man must establish a connection with God; he must establish a connection with his Father. He must acquire God's qualities and act with those qualities. He must distinguish between his own four hundred trillion, ten thousand different qualities and God's three thousand gracious qualities and His ninety-nine actions, conduct, and qualities. He must compare the one hundred and five million qualities of the karma of birth, that exist in the world, with God's qualities. He must check and observe those qualities, and then he will know which ones are crazy.

Who is crazy and in what way? Is it the world? Is it man? Is it his qualities, actions, or thoughts? Which section is crazy? When we understand what is crazy, we will know that there is only One who is not crazy and that everything else is crazy. We will understand that we, and everything else, are crazy.

One has hunger craziness, one is money crazy, one is love crazy, one is woman crazy, one is house crazy, one is crazy about tastes, one has acting craziness, one has the sixty-four sexual games craziness, and one is crazy for the sixty-four arts and sciences. One is husband crazy, one is wife crazy, and one is children crazy. One is desire crazy, one is clothes crazy, and another is makeup crazy. One is job crazy, one is education crazy, one is religion crazy, and one is race crazy. One is crazy about politics, one is crazy about praise, one is crazy about miracles, one is crazy about occult powers, one is crazy about yoga. One has a craziness to draw. One is crazy about gems. One is crazy about flying in the sky and one is crazy about boring into the earth.

One has relations and blood ties craziness, one has a father craziness, and one has a brothers and sisters craziness. One is crazy about gardens, one is crazy about homes, one is crazy about temples, one is crazy about bathing, one is crazy about eating, one is crazy about travel, one is crazy about staying at rest houses, and one is crazy about going to bars. One is crazy about drugs, one has a craziness to take marijuana, another to take opium, and another to take LSD. One has a craziness to roam freely, one is school crazy, one has a craziness to be beautiful, one has a family craziness, one has a unity craziness, and another has a disunity craziness.

One has the craziness of wanting male children, while another has the craziness of wanting female children. One has homosexual craziness, one has lesbian craziness, and one has bisexual relationships craziness. One is crazy for solitude, one is crazy to be in the jungle, and another is crazy to be in the city. One has a craziness of wanting sex all the time. One has a craziness of hating everything. One has a craziness to build a house by the sea and one has a craziness to build a house in the forest. One has a craziness about having a house in the country and one has a craziness about having a house in town. One is crazy about living in freedom in the jungle or in the mountains. One has a craziness to live with animals, one has a craziness to live with lions, one has a craziness to live with elephants, one is horse crazy, and one is cow crazy.

Some are crazy to drink milk, some are crazy to eat meat, and some are crazy to eat vegetables. Some are crazy about gardening and some are crazy about farming. Some are crazy about cars, some are crazy about machines. Some are *vingnānam*, science crazy, some are *agnānam*, ignorance crazy. Some have a craziness about (intestinal) gas, some are crazy about bile, some are crazy about their body, some are crazy about performing. Some have craziness to live with animals, some are crazy about raising chickens, some are crazy about raising goats, some are crazy about breeding horses. Some are crazy to dig ponds. There are countless crazinesses like this. Some are bank crazy, some have a craziness to be important, wealthy, and great, and some have a craziness to do business.

Like this, there are countless crazinesses in the world. These are all the crazinesses of creation. All these countless crazinesses of creation roll together, enter man, and grab hold of his mind. When all of these thoughts enter and grab hold of him, he is crazy. Every thought is crazy. We must understand who has what kind of craziness and what kind of qualities. A human being must discover how many kinds of crazinesses exist within himself, how many kinds of crazinesses exist in the world, and what kinds of crazinesses others have. What is the craziness of suffering, what is the craziness of sorrow, what is the craziness of separations, what is the craziness of relations, and what is the craziness of family?

Having first understood what kinds of crazinesses exist within himself, and having understood what is within God, man must cure his own craziness by taking within himself the peace that is within God. He must check everything, and if he can find peace within himself, that will be exalted learning. That is psychology, God's psychology.

If that love (the peace that is within God) comes into a man, he can easily understand the craziness of the world and the craziness in man—the craziness of all beings. Once peace, love, compassion, patience, justice, and conscience come into him, and once God's truth and goodness grow within him, he can help others. Then he will understand that love, compassion, justice, patience, *sabūr*, inner patience, and *shakūr*, contentment, are the medicines that are needed to treat the illnesses of others. Understanding this, he will have no need to ask a person what illness he has. He will assess and know each illness. He can see this by observing how the face is. Is it tired, is it drawn? How is the vision in the eyes? How is the countenance? How are the teeth? How is the body? How is the mind? He can immediately observe all of this for himself.

If there is a mirror and a man goes and stands in front of it, what does the mirror do? It shows his reflection. Similarly, if you have an illness, and go in front of (one who is) a "mirror," the mirror will see that illness. The mirror sees that there is an illness and, after understanding the illness, shows love and compassion and gives the necessary solace and patience to cure that illness. That love can cure the illness, that comfort can cure the illness.

No matter what illness or disappointment there is, it is your love that can cure it. No matter how a craziness came, it is your love and your support that are the cure. Your love, your comfort, your happiness, your compassion, your speech, and your words must change hatred. No matter what has disappointed him, no matter what hatred he has, no matter what has afflicted him or worn him out, you will be able to see that state. Then your love must comfort him. Patience, love, compassion, tolerance, peace, and justice must embrace him. God's qualities must embrace him. It is your love that can transform that hatred, that divisiveness, and that illness. That is God's psychology.

Man's psychology is: If you join with God and make that love and faith grow, then you will have those qualities. If you have those qualities, then no matter what hatred there is, no matter what divisiveness there is, no matter what craziness there is, that hatred can be transformed, those differences can be transformed. It is the qualities of love that can transform them.

In the same way that God knows the heart and does His work accordingly, one who dwells in God's qualities and actions will know in his heart what is wrong with a person. He will not need to ask what is wrong. He will know what the illness is, where it came from—whether it is from the heart, body, eyes, legs, nose, *qalb*, inner heart, hands, or legs. He will know this immediately. He will know where the illness is located. He will understand its cause.

According to that, he must give love, wisdom, and comfort. He must speak lovingly and show love and embrace with love. This is not the embrace of the body, but it is the embrace of the heart, the embrace of compassion, the embrace of patience, the embrace of *sabūr*, inner patience. It is with these he must change that hatred and those differences. No matter what has caused the change in the person's heart, these qualities can transform it. That is God's psychology, and that is the psychology of a man who is joined with God. He must find the cause of the person's mental anguish and sorrow and transform it with understanding, love, and compassion. These are the qualities that can change this.

It is not (ordinary) medicine that cures; it is the medicine of wisdom, love, and grace that is the cure. Medicine is only a small part of it. Love, God's qualities, compassion, conscience, and trusting other lives as your own are the true medicine. It is not necessary to ask what is wrong; it will be understood before asking. That is psychology, God's psychology. That is the work that God does.

If a man comes to this state and knows this, he will be a psychologist, a representative of God's psychology. If he wants to find a way to cure these mental illnesses, then he must know that Love is God, that good duty is exalted, and that good and peaceful qualities are the cure of illness. Medicine plays just a small part. Love is a great medicine, compassion is a great medicine, justice is a great medicine, patience is a great medicine, and conscience is a great medicine. God's qualities are the greatest of all medicines. If that medicine is given, it will end the illnesses of the world and the four hundred trillion, ten thousand kinds of crazinesses of the world. Everyone who has been born is crazy; their thoughts are crazy. The medicine to cure all this is love and compassion.

When a man develops this state within himself, he is a doctor, a psychologist, God's psychologist, God's representative. He can cure mental illnesses. If he can become one who can cure these illnesses, if he reaches that state, he can give peace to all lives. But first he must learn about that peace. What God has learned, what God has within Himself, man must learn within himself. He must study that Power within himself. He must establish that state within himself. If he wants to nurture goodness and peace within others, he must first cultivate and fertilize these crops within himself.

We are human beings. Let us look at how a gardener looks after tiny plants. If he is growing fruits and vegetables on his land, he must decide when to pull the weeds, how much fertilizer to add, how often the plants should be watered, and how often they should be sprayed with insecticides. Each crop must be planted in the correct season. The gardener must know how much time is needed for this, how much time is needed for that—how much time is needed for a seed to grow—how much time is needed for corn, how much time is needed for beans, how much time is needed for cabbage, for potatoes, for soybeans, and for rice. He must know how much time is needed, is that not so? He must give the necessary insecticides and water, and plant and grow the different seeds according to their needs and according to the time that is required, is that not so?

While apple or pear trees are still small, a gardener plants them and wraps them in cloth to prevent them from being damaged by rain or snow. He wraps these saplings round and round with a cloth to protect them, does he not? Similarly, we must wrap the illnesses of our brothers and sisters, in our love. By wrapping them in love, by wrapping them in compassion, and by wrapping them in good qualities, we can protect them from being attacked and damaged by illusion, desire, karma, faults, anger, darkness, and arrogance. In the same way the gardener wraps and protects the saplings, in the same way he tends and protects the seeds and seedlings, in the same way he protects the trees, and in the same way he protects the grass and the crops that provide food, we must care for and give peace to others. We must do it in the same way he does. To cut away each illness, we must cut away what is bad and develop what is good, the good qualities. Just as we grow crops to give us benefit and profit, we must cut away disease and make goodness grow for the benefit of other lives. Those qualities will give good benefit.

Consider how many potatoes grow from one seed and how a small apple seed produces a thousand apples. Like this, we must have the state and qualities that will dispel the suffering of others and bring them to a state where they, in turn, can give benefit to others. A gardener cultivates his crops and tends the trees, grass, plants, and shrubs in a way that brings them to a state where they can be of benefit. Psychology is like this. A man's psychology is like this. We must work hard with our bodies, wealth, and souls, so they can benefit others. Then we must offer this goodness to all mankind. That is the state in which this psychology must be done. This is the psychology of God's family, and we must do this with faith in God and His qualities.

A healer, a doctor, a psychologist, a human being, a shaikh, a guru—one who has this state is a guru, one who has this state is a psychologist, and one who understands these qualities is a doctor. One who acts from this state has the qualities of man and God. He is a human being, *mānidan*. He has established goodness within himself. His treatment, wisdom, comfort, and qualities will end the crazinesses of others and make them peaceful and tranquil. We who are human beings must learn and understand this within ourselves. With faith and certitude in God and in ourselves, we must learn the wisdom which can understand this. We must, within ourselves, learn wisdom and understand that God is Love, understand that justice is God's kingdom, and understand that unity and equality are the story of our life. We must understand that we are all one race, that we are all the children of Adam ☺.

There is only one God. God is One, and He is our Father. We must bow down to Him and show Him respect. We must follow Him, love Him, have faith in Him, and acquire His qualities. We must change into children who will perform His duties. If we transform ourselves in this way, we will become those who can serve others and help end the world's disease and mental illness. We will become God's family of psychologists, doctors, wise men, shaikhs, and good men.

As long as we fail to understand this state, we are crazy, the world is crazy, and all of creation is crazy. There is nothing that is not crazy. Our craziness is the same as the craziness of others. The world is crazy, creation is crazy. Everything is crazy except God. Everyone has arrogance craziness, karma craziness, pride craziness, jealousy craziness, vengeance craziness, race craziness, and countless crazinesses like these. Everyone is crazy; everyone is a crazy person, except God and Truth. Therefore, we must study this and know it. You must know what is wrong and change into a physician who can cure mental illness. Then you will be a psychologist, a doctor, a wise man, and a shaikh.

Whatever part of creation you praise, whether it is yoga, *gnānam,* occult powers, miracles, doctors, titles, psychologists, scientists, kingdoms, or politics—whatever you praise, this praise is just a craziness. Every quality is a craziness, every action is a craziness. We will be crazy until we understand and learn this—until God comes within us, until we take in and realize His qualities, His actions, and His kingdom. We will be crazy until we understand the difference between the world and God, until we distinguish between their actions, cut away the actions and qualities of the world, and act as God acts. Please reflect on this. This is the meaning of mental illness.

It would take many years to finish speaking about this subject. This is a vast history. It would take many yugas to say all there is to say about God, man, craziness, maya, and desire! I have spoken of it very briefly today. Man needs to think about this.

How should human beings give treatment? Love is God, and it is this Love that is needed to cure illness. In order to cure illness, understanding is needed. We must try to learn how to give peace to all creations. One who has come to the state of being a man, a psychologist, a doctor, a guru, or a shaikh will be able to end mental illness. When he acquires God's qualities of compassion and love, he will be able to end the illnesses of others.

Everyone is crazy. God considers everyone to be crazy. Why? Because we are not with Him. That is the illness. That is why the world is crazy. Everything is crazy. Every creation has the craziness of attacking, killing, and eating another and of trying to capture the kingdom of another. We must think of this. This craziness is mental craziness.

We will speak about the craziness of *gnānam*, divine wisdom. (What we are speaking about now) is the craziness of the mind. We need to speak about *gnānam* craziness. We will speak later.

A'ūdhu billāhi minash-shaitānir-rajīm.
I seek refuge in God from the accursed satan.

Bismillāhir-Rahmānir-Rahīm.
In the name of God, the Most Compassionate, the Most Merciful.

Raise the Children with God's Psychology

March 7, 1982, Sunday 10:47 AM

We must think about the psychology teachings of God. When you say psychology, it means to understand the attachments of the mind. It is to understand the way the attachments of the mind work, to take the meaning, and to dispel what is evil. What is known as psychology is (to understand) the attachments of the mind. Just as a magnet pulls iron towards it, one mind must enter another mind and understand the attachments that are there. The mind that is like a magnet must pull the tired mind that is like the iron towards it. Just as a magnet connects, this should connect. The magnet must take hold of the patient's *qalb,* inner heart, merge with it, and understand what is within it.

In the same way that iron, when put into fire, is changed into fire, the mind of the psychologist must go into the mind of the patient and, having entered it, must transform the patient into his beautiful qualities. With that faith, with God's qualities, with the qualities he has learned from Him, with the qualities he has acquired from Him, he should change the patient. With God's qualities, he should change all the suffering in the patient's mind, just as fire changes iron. He should truly change him. When that change is complete, it is fire, just as the iron is changed into fire.

Then the thoughts of the patient can be shaped to the side that he wants. God's qualities must go and do that.

God's grace is the magnet. It goes into the patient's *qalb* and grasps it. It grasps the *qalb,* just as a magnet grasps hold of iron. That love grasps it. That grace, love, and wisdom take hold of it, and when they capture that heart, they change it just as fire changes iron when the iron is put into it. It is in this way that God's qualities, wisdom, and that love must enter and transform the mind, which is like iron. God's qualities and grace must come and give the explanation in order to change the illness. When it is changed, it (the heart) becomes like the fire. Then it is fire. When it is changed in this way, it becomes the qualities of God, and the illness leaves. When it becomes God's love, that illness leaves. When it becomes God's grace, that illness leaves. What will it be like? In that state, what will happen?

When a flower blooms and becomes beautiful, a fragrance permeates every petal, does it not? When a rose blooms, each petal has a fragrance. Each petal that is plucked has a fragrance, does it not? You can smell that fragrance in every petal. The fragrance beckons us, the scent of the flower calls us.

Similarly, once we reach this state and the beauty of the *qalb* develops, once the beauty of His qualities comes, then the light of God's grace, that fragrance of grace, enters that *qalb.* When the flower of the *qalb* blooms, when evil leaves and the plenitude of good qualities comes, that fragrance comes. Just as every petal has a fragrance, every thought has a fragrance, every look has a fragrance, every yearning has a fragrance, every intention has a fragrance, every action has a fragrance, and every behavior has a fragrance. Fragrance permeates our conduct, behavior, and love.

Then the heart will be a rose flower. Its fragrance will give peace to all lives. That fragrance is a cooling fragrance, a fragrance of love, a fragrance of peace, a fragrance of tolerance, a fragrance of patience—the fragrance of God's qualities.

If one can change his own nature, if he can develop those qualities and then change the qualities of others, then that is psychology. A connection to the heart must be established. These questions should not be asked: "What did you do? Did you make love? Do you like sex? Do you like your husband? Do you like dramas? What happened there? How do you feel towards your child? How did you sleep? How did you sit? How did you do that? Tell me what you said." These are not the correct questions. "How did you leave? What happened?" What I spoke about earlier is the point. This is not something that should be spoken of aloud. There is no need to ask questions about things that have happened on the outside.

This is psychology: If man learns the qualities of God, he will understand that it is not necessary to ask questions. There is only the medicine to be given, the medicine of love. That medicine must be given. You must take hold of the mind, give it that medicine, and transform it.

But instead of doing this, each day the patient lies on a couch with his eyes closed, talking about sex, talking about pleasure, and about how he slept, how he sat, how this happened, or how that happened.

"Divorce that person, that person is not good. Divorce that person, that person has faults. That husband is not good for you. That wife is not good for you." These are not (appropriate) questions.

The earth can give gold. The earth can be made into something beautiful and can give something beneficial, something that is valuable. The earth is without fault. What was once earth can be cleared, made into gold, and given as a valuable metal. But as long as it stays in the earth, it remains earth. If you extract copper or mercury from the earth and change it, it can be made useful.

Like that, do not say, "Get a divorce, he is not good for you, she is not good for you, he is not suitable for you." It can be *made* suitable. Instead, the qualities that are unsuitable have to be removed. That is the treatment. Just as gold is taken from the earth and is made useful, just as land that is not fertile is cultivated and made useful, just as a barren tree is made to bear fruit, the mind that has been caught in the entanglement of illusion must be made clear. The mind should not be cut away, but should be made clear.

This is God's teaching, His psychology. Man must reach this state of wisdom. Only this state is psychology, the psychology of one who is a man. We must think about this. We who are human beings must think of this and understand what we need to learn. It is through the connection to God that we must learn this, and then give peace to the people by giving this explanation. That is the exalted learning. Let us think about it. *Āmīn.*

Now we will speak further. How should a teacher be? How should a mother be? How should a mother, who has given birth to a child, raise this child? When a man and woman are conducting their lives, four hundred trillion, ten thousand different qualities, desires, the sexual games, and the arts and sciences can enter their minds. The mind is a place where these dwell. The mind is a jungle where snakes, scorpions, eagles, vultures, tigers, elephants, fanaticism, differences, deer, elks, goats, cattle, donkeys, horses, dogs, foxes, wolves, cats, and rats dwell, where countless reptiles, scorpions, snakes, birds, animals, and monkeys dwell. They dwell in this jungle.

In this jungle there is also a beautiful house, the inner heart, the *qalb*—God's house. That is a subtle house. Before we can reach that house, we must cross the jungle that surrounds it. All the animals, demons, and ghosts live in this jungle. It is filled with these poisonous beings and dangerous animals. We have to go through this jungle. We will encounter animals, illusion, darkness, torpor, mesmerism, magic, occult powers, miracles, the "I" and "you," and the miracles of flying, walking on water, walking in the sky, walking below, and walking on fire. All these miracles are there. The five kinds of lives dwell in this jungle, but *pahut arivu,* divine analytic wisdom, and *pērarivu,* divine luminous wisdom, are not there. *Pahut arivu,* the understanding of right and wrong, is not there.

The sixty-four sexual games and sixty-four arts and sciences are playing in the thoughts. These are the *līlai vinotham* and the *kalaigal,* the sixty-four arts and sciences and the sexual games. It is within these sexual games that the qualities and essences of the animals are joined. They are mingled in the blood, in the flesh, in the bones, in the marrow, and in the nerves. All these qualities are mingled in the body when the fetus is formed. When a child is born, he arrives with this connection. This is karma. This is not an earlier karma, but comes from the connection to the fetus when the fetus is formed. When you are born, this karma comes with you, and it develops and grows as you grow.

In what way can the mother and father cut this (karma)? They must understand how they should bring up their children. (First,) they must get rid of all their own faults and everything that is joined to them.

If you have a male child you have to think, "This child sleeps the same way we slept. He grabs and bites the same way I did. He walks the way I walked. Is it wrong or is it right?" We must understand this. "He is rolling the way we rolled. He is doing what I did. He is crawling the same way I crawled on two legs and two hands.

This is what I did. That is wrong. Although I did this without him knowing it, he is now revealing it, he is exhibiting it outwardly. He is showing what I did (earlier). All right. I lived with only one husband, (or) I lived with only one wife, but he is holding everyone the same way I held that one wife or husband. He holds onto the breast of everyone, he holds onto the eyes of everyone, he holds onto the nose of everyone, he bites everyone's cheek. What I did with one person, he is doing with so many. I slept only on the lap of my wife (or) I slept only on my husband's lap, but he sleeps on everyone's lap. I only bit once, but he is biting everywhere. What I did one time, he is doing many times. Ahhha! This is wrong. I did one thing, and he is doing it in many different ways. This is wrong, these qualities are wrong."

The mother and father must think, "Whatever we said earlier, he is saying now. He started talking. He started walking. He is staggering in the same way I staggered when I was drunk. He is showing me everything I did. The way I stole, he is trying to steal. The way I grabbed, he is trying to grab. Whatever I did earlier, he is now showing me." They should think of this, "Oooh, oooh! This is wrong."

First one must correct oneself, and then correct the child. With love we must teach good speech. The parents must learn good speech and then teach that good speech to the child. The parents must live their lives on the straight path and then teach their child to live on the straight path. The parents must be happy and teach their child to be happy. First you must teach yourself, and then you can teach the child (good) qualities, speech, vision, thoughts, love, compassion, patience, and tolerance. You must teach the child these. You must teach him (or her) peacefulness. You must teach him how to comfort. You must teach him in this state.

Every quality you have is recorded by the children. Whatever you do, they absorb; whatever you say, they absorb; whatever you look at, they look at; whatever sound you make, they make that sound. When you are talking or when you not talking, they absorb that sound. Therefore, if you do everything in a beautiful way, they will also do everything in a beautiful way.

If you display beautiful qualities, they will display beautiful qualities. If you speak beautiful wisdom, they will speak beautiful wisdom. If you speak beautifully about faith in God, that child will have faith in God. If you speak beautifully about unity, that child will have unity. If you demonstrate equality in a beautiful way, the child will also demonstrate equality in the same way. When you act according to your conscience, explaining this to the child, he will also act according to his conscience. If you speak with justice, the child will show that justice. If you show a smiling face, the child will show a smiling face to everyone. If you show a hard face, the child will show a hard face. If you show anger, the child will show anger.

Like this, the parents must learn this good state and show it to the child. Then the child will learn. In this state, a mother and father are the guru. Before the child goes to school, the parents have to train him. What the mother and father teach the child in the cradle, what is learned while young, is like writing on stone. It is impressed on the child's *qalb*, inner heart. It is recorded. If you do not tell a lie, the child will not lie. If you do not backbite, the child will not backbite. Whatever you do, he will do. Therefore, if you do what is good, if you behave in a good way, he will behave in a good way.

If the husband and wife bite like cats and dogs, the child will learn that. Your child will develop in whatever state you are in. A mother and a father must teach the child the good state. First you must learn it yourself, and then show it to your children. You must grow in that way, and then show them how to grow in that way. You must have equality, and then show this to your children.

Like this, the mother and the father should demonstrate good thoughts to their children. If you show them differences and prejudice, that is how they will behave. Everything is taught by the parents, whether it is good or bad. What comes from the parents is picked up by the children. If the mother and father teach them the good way, the children will be good. That is how you raise a child. That is a good mother, a good father, God's family, one that shows and teaches God's qualities, peace, conscience, justice, and patience.

A mother and father who raise their child to a good state are God's family. By speaking without speaking, teaching without teaching, showing without showing, they must demonstrate the good path. You should think of this. Then, whatever karma the mother and father gave to their child earlier will be cut off. As a result, you can become good, and your child can become good. You must learn what is good from your child, and your child must then learn to be good from you. If you understand this, you will be able to learn from the child. Once you have understood it from the child, then the child will, in turn, learn from you, and will become a good child. You must think about this. Every mother and father should think about this.

How should a teacher be? A teacher who brings up a child is like one who prepares and cultivates a jungle or barren land. If a jungle is cut, tilled, and fertilized, if different crops are planted, watered, fertilized, sprayed with insecticides, and protected, it will bear good crops or fruit.

The child comes to a teacher at the time he is without wisdom, at the time he does not know the difference between right and wrong, at the time he does not know what snake has poison and what snake does not have poison, at the time he does not know the difference between good food and bad food, at the time he does not know the difference between sweet and sour, at the time he thinks that sweet is sour and sour is sweet, at the time he is playful and thinks good is bad and bad is good. That is the time the child goes to school to learn from the teacher.

How should that teacher be? The mother gave milk from her breast, but the teacher must give the milk of love, the milk of love and compassion from the heart. With God's qualities, the teacher must give the milk of love from the heart. Just as the mother gave milk from her own flesh, the teacher must give the milk of love. With soft words, gentle love, melting love and kindness, with a look of grace and with a smiling face, the teacher must give the milk of love to the child from the heart. This is the milk the teacher must give. By giving this milk, the child can develop.

Doing this is like cutting down a jungle that is filled with animals and snakes. It is like felling trees, clearing the jungle, and making that jungle into a beautiful flower garden. It is like making it into a farm by planting it with beautiful fruit trees, beautiful vegetables, crops, and flowering trees. If we toil with so much difficulty to make a jungle into a garden or a farm, can we not also do this for our children?

Is it possible to prune a tiny plant with a huge knife? If you cut a tiny plant with a huge knife, it will die. If you puncture a tuber, it will die. The correct amount of manure, the correct amount of water, and the correct amount of insecticides must be used on each crop. If you exceed the limit, the crop will die; if you give it too little, the crop will not grow; if you give it too much, it will die. There is a limit. We must grow these crops with love and give what is needed according to that limit. We cannot get angry at the plant. It grows by love, it grows by the love of our hearts.

In the same way that we toil so hard to clear the jungle of the grass and weeds, and then plant crops and trees, we have to raise children with love and devotion. We must destroy the jungle of ignorance in their hearts, and then plant the crops of love, the crops of grace, and the crops of wisdom, developing good qualities and actions. Just as there is a limit to what we give each crop, we have to give each child what he needs, in accordance with his limit and the time it is needed. Wisdom and good qualities must be measured and given according to what is needed, just as we limit the water given to a crop. The child will grow and develop if we give good qualities and good actions at the time they are needed.

Just as we grow a plant lovingly, giving manure, insecticides, and water according to its limit, in this state a teacher should raise the schoolchildren with love, compassion, patience, tolerance, peace, *sabūr*, inner patience, *shakūr*, contentment, *tawakkul*, trust in God, unity, and exalted qualities. It is with these qualities of God that the plants will thrive. These (children) are the crops that are grown in school. They are the beneficial crops that can be made useful to many. The teacher must be in the state where she can develop these crops in the correct way, raise them with love, and show them love.

If you get angry at a plant, if you let it dry out, if you give it too much or too little insecticide, it will die. If you show differences, it will die. According to its limit, you must show it the correct amount of love, give it water, and cultivate it.

What God does for everyone is like this. Our Father acts in this way. If the teacher can raise her children like this, they will be crops that can be beneficial in many different ways. They will do so much good. They will be children who give peace to other lives. They will succeed in their own lives and other lives will succeed. These children will love other lives, they will have love in their own lives, and they will show that love to others.

This is what a teacher must do. If a teacher understands this, if he or she understands this kind of learning and understands these qualities, man would never become an animal; man would never be evil. They (the children) will grow in love, give love, show love, mature in love, flourish in God's qualities, and grow to be of great benefit to everyone. They will have justice and conscience. Those crops will grow in this good way. Just as a jungle is cleared to grow good crops, we must raise the child with love and allow his natural goodness to develop. God is like this. (Even) the grass and the weeds grow this way.

If a teacher raises the children in this way, if the children develop in this state, they will not be spoiled. The teacher's qualities should be God's qualities. She must have God's actions, God's behavior, God's conduct, God's love, and His three thousand gracious qualities. If a teacher is filled with love and has a smiling face, a loving face, a face that embraces—if she has an open heart, a melting heart, and if she protects the children, embraces them, and teaches them with wisdom—then those children will change into human beings and will later do service to God and service to the people.

A teacher should think of this. Teachers are those who give wisdom, who give love, and who guide the children on the path of life, and they should think about this. Having considered this, both teachers and mothers should act accordingly.

If the world is to be saved and if humanity is to flourish and survive, the mothers, fathers, and teachers must come forward and do their duty properly. What is destructive or what is constructive, good or bad will result from the way you do your duty.

Mothers, fathers, and teachers should think of this.

Thinking of this, we should take on God's qualities and actions and have faith in God, saying that God is only One, that there is only one family, that God is the only One worthy of worship, that God's actions are without any fault or craziness. We must then eliminate all the crazinesses. If we do our duty with the intention of doing good, then the children, the country, and all the people will live in freedom, and there will be happiness, peace, and equality.

May we think of this. We will speak more about this later. Tiredness has come.

A'ūdhu billāhi minash-shaitānir-rajīm.
I seek refuge in God from the accursed satan.
Bismillāhir-Rahmānir-Rahīm.
In the name of God, the Most Compassionate, the Most Merciful.

A Pure Human Being Can Dispel the Darkness of Birth

March 9, 1982, Tuesday 6:15 AM

Bismillāhir-Rahmānir-Rahīm. In the name of Allāh, the Most Compassionate, the Most Merciful.

Precious jeweled lights of my eye, brothers and sisters, we spoke earlier about psychology, Allāh's psychology. We spoke earlier about two or three sections. Now we are going to speak about the section of an Insān Kāmil, a pure human being.

An Insān Kāmil is one who, in this form, this *sūrat* of man, has changed into a human being. He has changed into a man and understands man. He shows that there are (two types of beings), *insān-hayawān,* man-animal, and *hayawān-insān,* animal-man. One is a man who is like an animal and the other is an animal that is like a man.

One (man-animal) may look like a man, but inside he has the five elements, mind and desire, the qualities of the animals, and the qualities of the elements. His mind is like that of a monkey, and he has the qualities of the dog of desire. He has the many qualities of all the creations—of earth, fire, water, and air. He has the shaktis, energies, of the earth. He has four hundred trillion shaktis—the shaktis and qualities of birds, four-legged animals, and reptiles, the shaktis and qualities of fire, water, air, ether, the

45

sun and the moon, and maya. Like this, he has all of these qualities within him. Because of these qualities, he will not understand
what is clean and what is unclean. His form will be that of a man,
but his actions and qualities will be those of an animal or a reptile.
This is how he lives. He is seen as a man, but all his inner actions
are those of an animal, a man-animal, *insān-hayawān*.

He should change from this section of an animal, *hayawān*,
into a man, an *insān*. If he changes this section, he becomes an
insān. If he has changed into an *insān* and knows the explanations
of that, he will know the difference between *hayawān* and *insān*.
He will understand both. Understanding this, instead of being an
animal himself, he will come to the state where he can understand
how to control and herd all the animals that are inside him; he
will be like a cowboy. He must develop the ability to do this. If he
develops this ability, he can control and herd these animals and
poisonous beings that are trying to eat him. If he has developed
like this, he has changed into a human being.

He must clear what is inside him. He must clear and open out
that animal form, that *hayawān sūrat*, that is inside him and become a shepherd, an *insān*, who controls this. If he becomes like
a shepherd who can control and herd these (animals), then he is
called a human being, an *insān*.

After he becomes an *insān*, he must change into an Insān
Kāmil, a pure human being. Once he becomes an Insān Kāmil,
he will be able to subdue and control all the shaktis that try to
enchant him, the earth, fire, water, air, and ether, illusion, torpor, and darkness, the shaktis that can fascinate him, the miracles, mantras, mesmerisms, magic, tricks, and occult powers, the
shaktis that emerge from earth, water, air, fire, and illusion, from
the sun and the moon, from the dog of desire, from the monkey
mind, and their explanations.

If, with the power of the soul and with the Power of God, he changes and controls these torpors, in that state he is an Insān Kāmil. When he cuts away the torpor and changes those states, he is an Insān Kāmil. He becomes God's representative, one who has received the complete powers of wisdom. He has the ability and the state to control the world and everything in the world. He is an Insān Kāmil. He is called a Kāmil, a representative who has a connection to Allāh. That representative can control all the energies, the torpors, and the qualities of the children he is raising.

According to that meaning, he understands wisdom, the complete wisdom, God's wisdom, God's qualities, God's actions, God's conduct, behavior, and love, and the state of the four different paths that he travels in his life: surrender, perfect balance, absolute focus, and divine wisdom, *tānam, nidānam, avadānam, gnānam.* He walks on that path. He walks on the path of wisdom, and acquires the four qualities of modesty, reserve, shyness, and fear of wrongdoing, *nānam, madam, atcham, payirppu,* and protects himself with them.

One who has attained this state is an Insān Kāmil, he is known as a Shaikh. On the outside he is called a Shaikh. It is rare to find such a one in the world. It is rare to find in the world one who has controlled all these shaktis. He is a man. He has changed into a human being. Among mankind he has attained exaltedness. He exists as *insān,* as Insān Kāmil.

He can control all the shaktis. He can control the torpors, the energies, and the miracles. To the world he is a power, a light. He is like a sun to the world. He can work in both sections: the section of darkness and the section of God. He can give clarity to those who are immersed in the torpor of this world, and soothe them. He can help relieve them of their torpor. He will be like a sun in the world, helping those who have faith and certitude to go on the straight path. He will be a light to those who are dwelling in the section of night. And to those who are dwelling in the section of light, he will be an *oli,* an even brighter light, a *velichcham,* a resplendence. Both sections are in his control.

In the section of light, he cuts the torpor of the clouds, lightning, and thunder. Seven kinds of clouds are running inside man. These are the inner attachments. There are many attachments inside that must be cut, the attachments of the blood. The Insān Kāmil can cut these. Even those who have faith, certitude, and determination have differences of religion, colors, hues, blood ties, attachments, the ego of the "I," arrogance, karma, and illusion, and the karmic connections. These connections are like clouds that are running within. Even one who has faith, certitude, and determination wavers and is shaken as soon as sorrow comes. He wavers and is shaken because of these connections and because of mind and desire. At that time, just as the sun disperses the clouds, the Insān Kāmil will be the sun and disperse these clouds. He will give light to the seven kinds of desires, *nafs,* that are running inside and causing torpor. He will give wisdom. He will give that wisdom, those qualities, and those actions and show man the light of the freedom of the soul. He will open the path to freedom of the soul, and say, "This is the light. Look at it." And, for those who have been caught by illusion and who have fallen into darkness, the Insān Kāmil will be like the moon in daytime. He will be in the world, reveal explanations of the world, and show how to find freedom. He will teach both sections how to clear themselves and remove the darkness, how to remove the darkness of life, how to remove torpor, and how to cut the connection of torpor.

One who can dispel the darkness of birth and give clarity to both sections is known as a Shaikh, an Insān Kāmil. He has God and God's qualities of *sabūr,* inner patience, *shakūr,* contentment, *tawakkul,* surrender to God, and *al-hamdu lillāh,* giving all praise to God. *Tawakkulun ʿalAllāh, al-hamdu lillāh.* His property is God, his property is God's qualities. He performs his duty and his actions with these qualities. For this reason, he is known as an Insān Kāmil. He is known as a Shaikh.

We will now talk about the four different ways in which man's form, his *sūrat,* is developed. Āndavan, Allāhu taʿālā Nāyan, is the Creator, the Supreme Being who resonates as Allāhu, as the *Nūr,* the Light, the Plenitude, the One who does not waver, the Complete Treasure. That is a Mystery, a Secret, a Power. As One who is without form or color, It remains as Itself, *aduvai aduvai endru.* That all-pervasive Allāhu is a great Power, the Creator. That Treasure gazes intently at all creations, and then creates.

Bismillāhir-Rahmānir-Rahīm. Bismin (is) the Treasure that manifests on Its own and creates what appears. It is the Source, the Origin of what appears. That Treasure then makes it manifest. Whatever is intended, that Treasure intends within that intention, and fulfills it. Like this, that mysterious Power does countless things. That secret Power, which is without form, remains by Itself, alone, yet is mingled with everything, makes everything clear, makes everything move, and exists with the clear explanation that not even an atom would move without It. That Power is God. It is perfect Purity. It nurtures each creation according to its individual quality, according to the way it was created, and according to its nature. It brings each up according to its nature, its actions, and its state, and makes it useful.

He (God) created a sun, and uses its light and rays to give benefit. He created the snake, gave it poison, and uses the poison to remove another poison; He uses it as a medicine. He uses one poison to counteract another bad poison. He created the earth, and with the earth gives benefit to another portion of the earth. He created the grass, and with the grass gives comfort to another section of grass. He created a weed, and through it gives benefit to other things. He created a seed, and giving the necessary help to the seed, with it gives benefit to other creations. He created an elephant, and by developing its qualities, with it gives benefit to others. Like this, He created every creation. If something was created, He developed it to be of benefit to something else. He did not create anything to be harmful. This is the way He nurtures His creations.

That God, Allāhu taʿālā Nāyan, nurtures His creations in this way, with that quality. He created one to cure the disease within another. He created each with its own purpose, so that it could change the qualities, actions, and conduct of another, and protect it. That Father, God, has that state and nature.

He created six kinds of lives, and in that state, He nurtures them and protects them. In that state, He does His duty. He has beautiful qualities—the three thousand gracious qualities and the ninety-nine wilāyats, powers—and in that state He brings up all lives. His life is sabūr, inner patience, shakūr, contentment, tawakkul, surrender, al-hamdu lillāh, all praise to God, and good thoughts. With those good thoughts and good qualities, with sabūr, shakūr, and tawakkul, and with the qualities that embrace others without hurting them, He gives love to others, embraces them to His breast of grace, and protects them. He does duty without likes or dislikes. His speech and actions are one, they are unified with what He does. His actions, behavior, and thoughts are one and the same. Each of His states is good. He is known as Allāh.

Even though He has many tens of millions of names, He

is Allāh, the One who never diminishes even though each *qalb,* heart, takes from Him. He is the great Ocean of Grace that never diminishes, the Ocean of Wisdom, the Ocean of *Gnānam,* the Ocean of Wealth, the Ocean of the Soul, the Ocean of the Resplendence of the Soul, the Ocean of Resplendent Plenitude. From this ocean, He rules this entire kingdom and does duty without swerving from perfect justice. He is the One who raises and protects all of the beings in that kingdom.

Of the six kinds of lives, He has created man as the most exalted life. Man has been given the wisdom to know himself. He has been given the wisdom to know the truth. He has been given the wisdom to do what is good. He has been given a mouth with which to speak with Him. He has been given eyes with which to see Him. Within this mouth, he was given a tongue with which to speak with Him. Within this nose that smells the world, he was given another nose which can smell Him. Within these eyes that look at everything, he was given another eye which can see Him. Within these ears that hear all the sounds, he was given an ear which can hear His sounds. Within this *qalb,* inner heart, that can understand everything, he was given a *qalb* which can understand Him. Within this body he was given hands that can do everything, and within those hands he was given hands that can embrace Him. He was given legs that walk everywhere in the world, and within these legs he was given legs to walk on His path.

He was given seven levels of wisdom and the consciousness to understand everything, and within that wisdom he was given the wisdom of *gnānam* to understand Him. Within this hunger he was given the fire that burns everything, and he was also given the fire of *gnānam* to understand Him and to merge with Him. He was given the fire that does not burn or harm anything, the fire that does not burn but which merges with Him. He was given all these bodies, and was made to understand everything. And within this body, he was given His (God's) body, His perfected Light body. He was given a body that does not have flesh, skin, bone, earth, fire, water, air, and ether, a body that does not have any connections to these.

For the worldly life he has been given a body with the five kinds of lives, and he has also been given the sixth body, God's body, the body of His Power that does not have a connection to the others. He has been given a body that rules this world, and he has also been given a divine body that rules the heavenly world.

He was given ignorance, false wisdom, and science, so he could do the research of awareness, and he was also given true wisdom, His wisdom of *gnānam,* with which he could research the world of *gnānam*—the wisdom to research the world of the souls and the world of *gnānam*.

Like this, God, the Causal Creator, reveals the essence of these countless actions and exists as inner Perfection, giving clarity to perfected man. That Power who gives that clarity to him and nourishes him, is God. He is the One who is not seen, but is the One who sees everything. Man exists without seeing Him, but He, the Power, is God who makes man see. He sees everything, but exists as a Treasure that is not seen by man. He gives man the wisdom to see Him, raises him to become a man, and makes man speak with Him.

In this state, He created man from an atom, from a *nuqtah,* a dot, and made him into a fetus. When he is a fetus, He nurtures him and teaches him. He teaches him about the soul, the explanation of the soul, the explanation of His kingdom, and of how to speak with Him. At the time the (physical) body is being formed, God forms His body within that body. He forms His body within it and nurtures him (man) in this way.

He develops and teaches him for ten months in the womb. He opens the eye to see Him alone. The section of the world that the eyes see is cut off, and He gives him the eye to see Him. The sounds of the world that the ears hear are cut off, and He gives him the ears to hear His sounds. The worldly smells, the stench of blood that is within the womb, are cut off, and He gives him the nose that smells Him. He gives him a mouth that chews the hells of the world, and He gives him a tongue and mouth that savor His taste and speak with Him.

He gives him the hands that steal and grab in the world, and He gives him the hands of faith, certitude, determination, *īmān*, in Him, with which to embrace Him. He gives him the body that exists as the world within the world, and He gives him the body of *gnānam*, the Light body of the soul, that exists as God within God, and makes him know it.

He gives what can cut the hunger of this world, and He gives him *sabūr*, inner patience, *shakūr*, contentment, *tawakkul*, trust in God, *al-hamdu lillāh*, all praise to God, the food that intends Him. He gives him *tawakkulun 'alAllāh*, surrendering all into God's responsibility.

Like this, He gives him all the duties of the world, and within that He teaches him the ways of worship to gain the freedom of the soul, and the way to speak with Him, to hear Him, and to see Him. This is what happens in these ten months. This is not the learning that comes on the outside. He speaks to him inside the womb. This is how God teaches him. It is in this very *sūrat*, form, that He speaks to that *sūrat*. That is the way our Father explains and teaches and nurtures us. It is He who brings us up and teaches us in the womb. That is our Father.

He is the omnipresent Father, the Father of our soul, the primal Father, the One who creates, the One who protects, the One who sustains, and the One who later calls us back to Himself. He is Allāh, who gives the explanation that later we will see Him whom we saw earlier. This is our mysterious *sūrat,* our *sūrat* of *gnānam,* divine wisdom, the *sūrat* of light. We must understand this body that He teaches and nurtures within (the physical body).

Precious jeweled lights of my eye, this is psychology, the psychology He teaches us. He has opened out and shown His countless qualities and actions. God says, "You can see all this: My kingdom, the kingdom of the world, the kingdom of hell, the kingdom of heaven. Look within these and understand. Now, I am sending you out from here. When you go out, this is what you have to understand. This is the meaning of understanding your-self." Then, in the tenth month, He sends him out. This is the way God nurtured and taught him (for ten months).

Secondly, the worldly father, the mother and father raise him. In the first section, the Father (God) brought him up. The second section is the mother and father. They teach him about blood ties; they speak about differences of religion, about rela-tions, race, caste, colors, hues, and languages, about foods, the world, property, inheritance, and mind and desire. These con-nections are taught by the parents. This is the way they bring up their children. "This is your uncle, this is your brother-in-law, this is your elder brother, this is our house, this is our property, this is our place, this is our inheritance, this is our gold, this is our money, this is our farm." These attachments of blood ties, karmic attachments, and the attachments of the world are taught by the mother and father. This is the way the mother and father raise the child, the way they teach him (or her) about the world, the way they teach him about the connections of the karma of this world, and the way they raise his (physical) body.

The third father is the school. The guru, teacher, the father in that school gives the children explanations of the world, of the sections of the world. He teaches them about what they should do to feed their stomachs and about the worldly section of fame, positions, pride, and arrogance, and their value. Feeling, awareness, and intellect...He teaches the sections that belong to this intellect, *putti*. The scriptures and philosophies, vedas and vedantas, that are taught extend only up to the limit of intellect. Whatever intellect gathers is made into a book, everything in the book is made into teachings, all the teachings are made into the sexual arts, all the sexual arts are made into the arts, all the arts are made into the world, everything in the world is made into praise in life, all the praise is made into desire, desire makes man into a monkey, the monkey mind, and he is taught to do the tricks of this monkey. This is what the world teaches as the ideal of life.

This father teaches you that what your eyes see and your ears hear—the attachments to the world and the religions—are what will help you to acquire praise and titles from the world. Simply with words, each thing is made to appear like a god. All the emotions of the mind are made into gods. All the inner qualities and thoughts are brought out and made into gods. All the qualities of snakes, elephants, cats, rats, demons, and ghosts, all the many emotions and thoughts in the mind are brought out and shown as gods. "This is the world, this is your life. Know this." That father teaches you this. This is the second (step) in the world, where man changes into this and that. (During the time of) this third guru, the desire for earth, the desire for woman, and the desire for gold develop in him. The connections of arrogance, karma, and maya, or illusion, develop within him; the qualities of the sons of maya, *tārahan, singhan,* and *sūran,* develop; desire, anger, miserliness, attachment, fanaticism, envy, intoxicants, lust, theft, murder, falsehood—these seventeen explanations develop within him. These seventeen puranas[1] come into him, and he is changed into the form of illusion.

Then he is shown the section of female. Maya stands within this in its own form, and entices and captures him. When it captures him, it makes him live in the darkness of torpor, and in this torpor, he acquires the arrogance of "I, I, I," and the title of "mine." He learns occult powers, miracles, mantras, mesmerisms, colors, and sexual games. The woman who teaches these is another guru. She is another father.

In this state, that woman (maya, illusion) becomes a father. The *nafs ammārah,* base desires, and the qualities that are within him change into the mother that raises him. He grows with those qualities, he is brought up by those qualities, he changes into that state and grows with that mother, that father. He forgets all that he learned earlier while still in the womb, and considers what he is learning on the outside to be what will give him the freedom of the soul. He considers this to be freedom in life, and he grows in that state. He looks at the five "people,"[2] he smiles at the five people, is enchanted by the five people, and his life ends in the two sections of mind and desire. The changes occur in this state.

In this way, he grows in joy and sorrow, in profit and loss, and he suffers. He runs about, roams and suffers, unable to dispel his sorrows and suffering. Some keep on searching, some die, some commit suicide, some pray, some worship, some cry, some roam in the forest, some go crazy. Some are crazy in the country, some are crazy in the jungle, some are crazy in their own cage (body),

---

1. purana (T) Literally, an ancient story, a legendary tale or myth. In this discourse Bawa Muhaiyaddeen ⊖ is referring to the seventeen evil qualities in man as puranas.

2. The five "people": The parents; the school; woman or maya, illusion; attachments; the qualities in the mind.

and some are crazy in their life. There are ninety-six different crazinesses, and with these, they wander around in their life.

It is in this state that an Insān Kāmil is necessary. If one finds him, what will the Insān Kāmil do with this section? He will again teach what was taught earlier by God while one was in the womb.

(First) the mother and father brought him up as a baby, then the school brought him up as a baby, then earth and woman brought him up as a baby, after that the attachments within him made him into a baby and raised him, and after that the qualities within his mind raised him as a baby.

God raised him as a baby and made him able to see Him and speak to Him. Then everything else made him into another baby, then into another baby, and into another baby, and (one by one) brought him up. It is in this way that the Shaikh, the Insān Kāmil, must also make him into a baby and teach him and bring him up on this (good) path. He must raise this baby. He must again make him into a baby and raise him.

A'ūdhu billāhi minash-shaitānir-rajīm.
I seek refuge in God from the accursed satan.
Bismillāhir-Rahmānir-Rahīm.
In the name of God, the Most Compassionate, the Most Merciful.

Everything You Need to Know Is Within You

March 9, 1982, Tuesday 11:30 AM

An Insān Kāmil will show his children: What you read earlier in the books of the world, what you learned through books and by examples, *utāranam*[1]—through religion and through the principles, *ātāram*,[2] and examples that you studied earlier—are all just scenes, *kādchi*,[3] that you saw. This learning is something you held in your hand and absorbed into your mind. Whether it was from books, from the world, or from observation, everything you learned was shown as an example, was it not? You saw this learning as a wonder, you saw it as a benefit.

But the "book" you need to study now is not a book (like that). That (learning) does not exist in books. The connection between *insān*, man, and Allāh, the connection between truth, *insān*, and Allāh, has no connection to what you previously studied in books. It has no connection to the understanding you gained from those books. There is another book, a mysterious *treasury* book. That book, relating to *insān*, Allāh, truth, and their qualities, must now be studied.

---

1. *utāranam* (T) Example, illustration, proof, authority.
2. *ātāram* (T) Basis, foundation, support, security, protection.
3. *kādchi* (T) Scene, vision, sight, view, visible appearance.

From now on you must become a baby. To study this, you must become a baby to the Insān Kāmil, to the Shaikh, and be brought up by him in the same way a mother brings up her baby. This is the only way you will be able to study this. You must now try to understand the way he is teaching and nurturing you.

From now on you must read from this book. This book is the story of Allāh, who is a mystery. This mystery is the heart of the Shaikh. The Insān Kāmil's heart is the book. The heart of the Insān Kāmil is the *storybook.* In this book, you will be able to see your story and the story of everything, without form or shape, as the form of light. Everything (there) has life, every point has life, *hayāt.*

What you have learned up until now has no life. Your art has no life. What you studied has no life. Whatever you may have achieved or completed is like this—it is a story without life, it is art without life. That is not the story of God, it is the story of creation. From now on you are going to study the story of the soul, the good story. You must study this with the wisdom of divine luminous wisdom. You must study this with the wisdom of the *Qutbiyyat*[4] and the wisdom of the *Nūr,* Light.

You must become a baby. Now you must grow as an embryo within the Shaikh. You must be born from him and be raised by him. You must prepare yourself for this development. You must throw out everything you learned earlier. What was within your heart, within your *qalb,* within your body, within your thoughts, within your intentions, within your vision, within your breath, within your sound, within your speech, and within your taste— whatever you realized from those and thought was good or tasty,

---

4. *Qutbiyyat* (A) The state of divine analytic wisdom or *pahut arivu.* That is the sixth level of consciousness, the wisdom of the Qutb ☙, the wisdom that explains the truth of God.

whether it was titles or status or praise, whatever you thought was giving you happiness—these must be thrown out. When you have thrown these out, when both happiness and sorrow are discarded, then you can (begin to) study. This is the *soul psychology,* God's *soul psychology* study. This is the study within yourself. For this, the book is within you, the map is within you, the story is within you, and everything that must be realized is within you. This is the (true) story, the miracle.

All the miracles you performed on the outside through your earlier lessons are not miracles. They did not come from within, and you could not have realized anything from them. All the miracles or siddhis you performed through the shaktis, energies, of the earth, fire, water, air, and maya, through the shaktis of jinns, fairies, demons, satans, and demonic forces, through the shaktis of the mind, the monkey of the mind and the dog of desire, through the shaktis of the sun, moon, and stars, through the four hundred trillion, ten thousand spiritual[5] mantra shaktis and maya shaktis did not give you any satisfaction. They have given you a title that will destroy you. That title, pride, envy, anger, impatience, and hastiness have given you a life without peace. They have brought you to a state that has no equality, peace, or tranquility. That is the state that you have been living in.

The learning you are going to do from now on is one where you can realize peace, equality, and tranquility within yourself. Unity, recognizing other lives as your own life, recognizing your happiness as the happiness of others, recognizing your peace as the peace of others, and recognizing your hunger as the hunger of others is the learning in which all lives can join and live with

---

5. spiritual: Bawa Muhaiyaddeen ☺ distinguishes between spiritual which denotes the elemental body and the soul which is the nature of God.

you and study with trust and love. You will be able to see this miracle within yourself. The miracle is to realize this within. In your speech, vision, heart, face, and body, within and without, in your death and in your life, in your words, actions, conduct, behavior, love, qualities, and duty, you will have compassion, love, justice, and tolerance. Within your conscience and justice, you can receive this beauty. This is the learning through which you can realize peace and tranquility. You can see this peace within yourself.

The miracles you performed earlier were for the world, but you were unable to find the miracle within yourself. The world may have praised you, but you did not find the praise within yourself. Your beauty may have been seen by the world, but you did not see the beauty, light, and peace within yourself. You may have received an exalted name from the world, you may have ruled the earth, you may have ruled the sky, you may have performed miracles, you may have been a king, a slave, or a rich man, but in your heart and in your face, you did not have peace, equality, justice, light, or the plenitude of the kingdom of the soul. You did not have the miracle by which all lives could have seen that (state) within you, and become enamored with you, trusted you, and had affection for you. You did not realize or see that miracle.

The (real) miracle is for you to see this miracle within yourself. Understanding this miracle through your beauty, through your light, through your wisdom, and through your qualities is God's miracle. This is what you must study. You must learn this from an Insān Kāmil. The learning, the map, your life, and your history are within you. Therefore, in your journey, your actions, your behavior, your conduct, your nature, and in your words, this will be understood.

When that understanding comes, that is the miracle. When

this is seen, you will understand that your resplendence is greater than the light of seventy thousand suns and seventy thousand moons. Your light will resplend in the world, in the kingdom of God, and throughout the eighteen thousand universes. That sun will resplend in the eighteen thousand universes. That light and beauty will be seen by the *malaks,* angels, the *malā'ikat,* archangels, and all lives. That light will be seen in the day and in the night. That power, that light will be seen in the present and in the future, and everyone will believe in it.

From now on, you will learn this from the Insān Kāmil. May you reflect on this. This is psychology. This is the learning which one must learn within oneself—God's psychology. I will now speak about this.

That Insān Kāmil is going to relate certain things to you. Have you, for one second, realized peace from anything you have studied up to now? No. If you did not find peace, is this learning? Did you find tranquility? Did you have equality or equanimity? Is this knowledge? No. You do not have peace. So far, all you have done in this world is play a game of football for a prize, yet you have not received a prize within yourself. Because you have not received a prize, you are going hungry, you are sad, you are suffering, you are sorrowful. What kind of life is it if you are sad and suffering and if you are without peace? What is your life? Is it a life? Without peace, your entire life is suffering. You need to think of this.

The Insān Kāmil tells his children that the lessons one understands and studies within himself is psychology. These are lessons learned through wisdom, through the qualities of God, through His actions, and through His Power. That is a secret, a mystery, a mysterious study. You cannot see this on the outside, it is on the inside. I will explain a few things to you:

To truth, falsehood is opposite.

To good, evil is opposite.

To good intentions, bad intentions are opposite.

To wisdom, ignorance is opposite.

To prayer to God, making anything comparable (to Him)
is opposite.

To good actions, bad actions are opposite.

To good speech, bad speech is opposite.

To sweetness, bitterness is opposite.

To good sounds, bad sounds are opposite.

To a good fragrance, a bad smell is opposite.

To a good sight, a bad sight is opposite.

To a good heart, a bad heart is opposite.

To the kingdom of heaven, the kingdom of hell is opposite.

To conscience—falsehood and envy are opposite.

To patience, anger is opposite.

To *sabūr,* inner patience, and *shakūr,* contentment—
hastiness and impatience are opposite.

To compassion, selfishness is opposite.

To duty, the connections of blood ties are opposite.

To the sun—darkness and clouds are opposite.

To the moon, the night is opposite.

To the stars, the rays of the sun are opposite.

To man's truthful life—the thoughts of mind and desire
are opposite.

To truth—selfishness and ignorant justice are opposite.

To hunger—the fire of arrogance and karma are opposite.

Air is opposite to water.

Water is opposite to fire.

Truth is opposite to illusion.
To justice, compassion, patience, and equality—
the emotions of the mind, selfishness, attachments,
and relationships are opposite.
To the equality of God, separations are opposite.
To peace in one's life—earth, woman, gold, wealth, and selfish
attachments are opposite.
These are opposite to the kingdom of heaven.
To heaven, hell is opposite.
To wisdom, ignorance is opposite.
To compassion, avarice is opposite.
To a truthful life—arrogance, karma, and maya are opposite.
To the love of God—the qualities of the three sons of maya,
tārahan, singhan, sūran, and maya, itself, are opposite.
To the duties of God—desire, anger, miserliness, craving,
fanaticism, and envy are opposite.
To peace and tranquility—intoxicants, lust, theft, murder,
and falsehood are opposite.

In this way, God has created so many opposites. A shrub with
a beautiful smell is opposite to a shrub with a foul smell. A sweet
fruit is opposite to a sour fruit. A tiger is opposite to a deer. A lion
is opposite to a cow. A blade of grass called *arugam pullu*[6] is opposite to a strong elephant. The base desires, *nafs ammārah,* of a
man are opposite to the qualities of God. The connections of the
world are opposite to the path of truth, and to faith. The attachments to the world are opposite to faith. A cat is opposite to a rat,
a mongoose is opposite to a snake, and a snake is opposite to an

---

6. *arugam pullu* (T) A tiny grass that grows in the tropics. When an elephant's foot
gets caught in it, it trips because it cannot free itself.

eagle. In this way, there are countless opposites of good and evil in the world.

God has created good and its opposite. Why has He created good and evil? So that we can eliminate evil, do what is good, and nurture the crops of the earth. The poison of a snake can cure a poison or an illness in a man. A bad quality in a person can be cured or changed by its opposite, a good quality in another; *that* is the medicine that can be given. This is why there are countless opposites. An elephant is a huge creature, but if you can change its qualities, you can make it do good work. If you can change what is bad within it, it becomes useful. If you can research and find the way to use an opposite to change it, then you can make it into something good. Fire and water are enemies, but fire can be used to change the bad properties in water so that man can use it. If you plant good crops in the dirty soil, the soil can give good crops.

Like this, there is an opposite for each thing, one impure and one beneficial. One thing can be used to change another thing and make it beneficial. You can take anything, and with its opposite, you can change it and make it useful. Evil qualities can be changed into good qualities. Bad poison can be put to good use. If you do not do this, it will remain evil. If you do not understand this, evil will do evil, karma will act out karma, and anger will commit the murder of anger. If you change (what is bad) with something that is good, then it will do what is peaceful and patient. Like this, for each thing, God has created these opposites to show the difference between the two. Man has the opportunity to change bad into good.

This is one (point) in the study of psychology. This is God's psychology. God shows the opposites in everything in creation, and He gives the treatment for each thing. He treats ignorance with wisdom. He treats lack of wisdom with intellect, *putti*. He treats feeling, *unarvu*, with awareness, *unarchi*. He treats judgment, *madi*, with subtle wisdom, *nuparivu*. He treats divine analytic wisdom, *pahut arivu*, with divine luminous wisdom, *pērarivu*. He treats the seven kinds of *nafs*, base desires, with the seven states of wisdom. He treats everything in creation with compassion and love, and maintains plenitude in His kingdom. He has no opposite. Since He conducts everything in the correct way, He has no differences, no separations, nothing that is bad. He makes bad into good. He shows the examples of good and bad so that we can understand creation and ourselves.

Why has it been created like this? God says, "I have correctly maintained the balance between the opposites. Realize that to Me there is no fault (in creation). I keep everything in balance. I have shown you what is good and bad, and you have the state to change it. You can change it into the kingdom of heaven. The kingdom of hell and the kingdom of heaven are within you. If you understand the kingdom of hell and the kingdom of heaven that are within you, then you can change the kingdom of hell into the kingdom of heaven. If you change what is bad inside you, you will become good.

"In My kingdom I consider everything equally. I do not discard anything. I created everything. I have created and shown pairs of opposites: man and woman, light and darkness, truth and falsehood, good and bad. I have created these to show you. In My kingdom, I do My duty without differences. Equality exists. I have transformed (what is bad).

"Like that, if you, with equality, bring to a good state the four hundred trillion qualities that are within you, the eighteen thousand universes that are within you, and the evil attachments and the differences that are within you, then you will create a kingdom of heaven within yourself. That is heaven. If you develop My kingdom within you, that is heaven. I have given you the wisdom to change, and I have also given you all My qualities. I have given you all My duties. I have given you My ninety-nine duties and actions. I have given you My three thousand gracious qualities. I have told you to do what I do, know what I know, understand what I understand, act the way I act, and realize what I realize. Am I not living without death or birth? Live like that.

"I am showing you that you are capable of doing all that I do. I have realized peace within Myself, and you can realize peace within yourself. I have realized tranquility within Myself, and you can realize tranquility within yourself. I have realized equality within Myself, and you can realize equality within yourself. I have realized unity within Myself, and you can realize unity within yourself. I have understood everything within Myself, and you can understand everything within yourself. I have understood tranquility and compassion within Myself, and you can understand compassion within yourself. I understand all lives and do duty to them, and they praise Me. You, also, should understand and do duty to all lives, and they will also praise you."

Like this, He gives the explanation and shows you examples. He shows this by example in the heavens, on earth, in *awwal*, the time of creation, and *ākhirah*,[7] the hereafter, in the sun, moon, and stars, in human beings and animals, in the birds and reptiles, in the demons and angels, and in the jinns and fairies. "I have shown this in everything. If you are able to act in the way I act, that is My kingdom. To understand this is My kingdom. It is the kingdom of heaven." God demonstrates this. "If you can do what

---

7. *ākhirah* (A) The permanent kingdom of God, comprising both heaven and hell, that exists after the Day of Judgment; the Hereafter. Literally, that which exists after an appointed time.

I do, if you can reach the state of peace that I have reached, then that is your home—peace, heaven. That is My throne, My seat of justice; that is My throne and My kingdom. You are in the kingdom of hell, but you must make that into the kingdom of heaven. I have made the kingdom of hell into the kingdom of heaven, and I am happy. You see the kingdom of hell as the kingdom of heaven, and you are not happy." God shows this to you.

This is the lesson we must learn. Because you must learn all of this, you must from now on become students of the Shaikh. Now you must be raised by him. You must grow as an embryo within the Shaikh.

This is the state the Insān Kāmil is going to teach you from now on. He will teach these lessons without a book. Through examples, he will explain the basic principle, and will reveal plenitude. He will reveal peace and plenitude.

This is a mysterious study. We need to reflect on this. I will speak more later.

A'ūdhu billāhi minash-shaitānir-rajīm.
I seek refuge in God from the accursed satan.

Bismillāhir-Rahmānir-Rahīm.
In the name of God, the Most Compassionate, the Most Merciful.

God Talks to the Baby in the Womb

March 10, 1982, Wednesday 7:50 AM

The Insān Kāmil, who is the Shaikh, begins teaching his child, who is like a baby. He takes everything the child learned and studied earlier, everything he believed in earlier and thought was true, and one by one shows each of these to him. Everything the child learned previously will be shown to him through wisdom, as opposites: That is what you learned, but *this* is the truth.

With God's qualities, God's actions, God's duties, conduct, and behavior, with *sabūr,* inner patience, *shakūr,* contentment, *tawakkul,* surrender to God, and *al-hamdu lillāh,* all praise is to God, in every thought, the Shaikh will show, one by one, the way God governs His kingdom. He will show tranquility, peace, equality, and unity, that there is one family, one race, one God, and one prayer. He will show and explain the many differences and many kinds of learning.

There are so many tens of millions of different kinds of fruit trees, are there not? Each tree has fruits with a different fragrance and a different taste. Like this, a Kāmil Shaikh will reveal each and every section and show:

This is true. That is wrong, the opposite.
This is wisdom. That is ignorance.

71

This is good. That is bad.
This is right. That is wrong.
In this way, he will take everything that was learned,
and show it:

This is the soul. Those are the spirits.
This is the pure spirit. That is the impure spirit.
This is the light soul, man's soul. That is one of the
five kinds of lives.
This is the kingdom of earth. That is the kingdom of heaven.
This is the kingdom of *gnānam*, divine wisdom.
That is the kingdom of hell.
This is a human being. That is a man-animal.
This is one who is wise. That is one who is ignorant.
This is God, the King. That is a king in the world of illusion.
This is justice. That is injustice.
This is truth. That is falsehood.
This is happiness. That is sorrow.
This is (true) life. That is false life.
This is true happiness. That is false happiness.
These are good eyes. Those are bad eyes, false eyes.
This is the tongue that tastes (what is good). That is the tongue
of the body of the five elements.
This is good speech. That is bad speech.
This is a good heart. That is the mind of the five elements.
This is faith. That is bad faith.
This is the soul life that has a connection to God. That has
a connection to mind and desire.
This is the quality of man. That is the quality of the snake.
This is the quality of wisdom. That is the quality of the vulture.

This is the quality of the vulture that eats corpses. Those
are the human vultures that eat other lives.

There are, like this, four hundred trillion, ten thousand spiritual qualities. This is a good prayer, that is the prayer of the stork.[1]
This is meditation. That is the meditation of the snake. This is
God's Power. That is the power of a demon. Like this, he will
show you everything. He will show each section and give its explanation. When wisdom grows, he will show you that everything
you believed in earlier is wrong. When he explains this, you will
know that everything you previously thought was true, is false,
that whatever you learned earlier, is false. With wisdom, the
Shaikh will show its state and prove to you that what you thought
earlier was true, is false.

What you believed earlier as true and what you saw earlier
as God will be shown with wisdom to be false. Like this, with his
wisdom and actions, the Shaikh will show you each and every
thing. Using your body, he will analyze and explain it. Using your
life, he will analyze and explain it. He will take your life and explain it. He will take your food and explain: This is good food,
that is bad food. He will take your speech and show it to you.
From your learning, he will show you the wrong and the right.
From the vision of your eyes, he will show you the wrong and
the right. From the sounds that you hear with your ears, he will
show you the wrong and the right. From what your nose smells,
he will show you: This is a wrong smell, that is a right smell. From
the tastes that you savor, he will show you: This is a wrong taste

---

1. prayer of the stork: Bawa Muhaiyaddeen ☉ often refers to Eastern meditations
   that reflect a particular animal's nature. He makes it clear, however, that the most
   exalted behavior comes from being a true human being, and that imitating animals will not bring one to that state.

and that is a right taste. From your breath he will show you: This is a wrong breath and that is the good breath. He will show you your speech in this way. From your actions, he will show the wrong action and the good action. From your conduct, he will show you: This is good conduct and that is bad conduct. From your thoughts: This is a good thought and that is a bad thought. From your intentions: This is a good intention and that is a bad intention. From your mind: This is a good mind and that is a bad mind. From your *qalb,* heart: This is God's *inside qalb* and that is satan's heart.

From your prayer, *vanakkam:* This is good prayer and that is bad prayer. From your meditation, *tiyānam:* This is good meditation and that is bad, an opposite meditation. From the mantras that you learn: This is a good mantra and that is a bad mantra, a mantra that belongs to the elements, to the demons, and to satan. From your behavior: This is good behavior and that is bad behavior. He will show you the opposites in all of the four hundred trillion, ten thousand spiritual thoughts, actions, and intentions. From your birth: This is good and that is bad. From your body: This is your light body and that is the earth body of the five elements. This is the kingdom of heaven, and that is your life, the kingdom of hell. He will explain whatever he sees in you.

Like this, section by section he will explain—from your food, your thoughts, your intentions, your sight, and your body. He will show you the kingdom of heaven and the kingdom of the world, the kingdom of hell and the kingdom of God. He will explain the kingdom of justice and the kingdom of injustice. He will explain the (good) conscience and the ignorant, selfish conscience.

He will reveal this map to you as you follow behind him on this path. One by one he will point out: This is this and that is that. When you go behind him on this path he will say: This path is this, that path is that; this is a path that has deep ditches, that is a good path. This forest is inhabited by huge animals that are dangerous and poisonous, that forest is good. You are doing the siddhis, miracles, of the five elements and the miracles of the animals. You are fighting like the monkeys, and you have the actions of the birds.

Within a second you can see the section of the entire world. The other is the section of the animals.

This is the strength of the elephant in musth. The other (section) is the strength of the soul, of truth, and of wisdom—God's strength.

This is the strength of the bull with which you are carrying the world. The other is God, the one Point, the strong Point which rules all of the universes.

In order to gain name and fame in the world, you are meditating like a stork that waits to catch a fish. The other is God's meditation where the soul joins with the Soul.

You are meditating like a snake, drawing in air. The other is God's Light where the soul meditates on the Soul, where God meditates on God.

This is the quality of the rat that bores holes; in this world you do the work of the rat, boring holes of "my race, my religion, your race, your religion." The opposite of that is peace and tranquility.

You are closing your eyes and showing some tricks. But God never closes His eyes; He is always alert. Truth never closes its eyes, it is always watching.

You grow your hair long and travel about like a sannyasi or a swamiar. But God has no hair. The hair that you grow causes you sorrow. You shave it, it grows back, you shave it, it grows back; it grows and then you cut it. This causes sorrow, this is your sadness. God has no hair. Truth does not have this body or this hair. It is clear, without impurity. Therefore, there is no value (in growing hair). This is wrong, this will cut your purity.

Your purity is your serenity. Your happiness is your peace. Your meditation is unity, love, and harmony. Your conduct is God's kingdom, considering all lives as your own life. Your duty is to do service to all lives. Your food is the peace and tranquility of others. Every section is like this.

Your miracle, siddhi: if you fly in the sky...if you walk on water, you are doing what a fish does. Observe if this is the work of a man. This is not the work of a man; it is not the sign of a man. If you can see this (sign), then that is a miracle. For you to walk across all of the universes in one second is a miracle. You can view that as a miracle. But if you do what a fish does, where is the miracle? A snake lives in a hole and breathes air. If you live in a cave and breathe the air of the five elements, can you call that a miracle? That is the work a snake does. When the snake puts its head outside, it catches the first rat it sees.

The rat that stays in the hole catches the frog. You should live in your own cave. Let your wisdom connect with God and taste that. Your wisdom should connect with God and savor that. You should savor His Light. There is a difference between this and that. You try to walk without being seen by other eyes, but cells and viruses enter your body without you seeing them. So you are just doing the work of a virus. Is that a miracle? No, it is not a miracle. A demon enters your body in the form of air. Dust from the earth enters you, water enters you, air enters you, fire enters you. They travel from cage to cage. They penetrate you and work inside you. Heat rays enter you. If you do what they do, is that a miracle? It is not a miracle.

If you take ganja, marijuana, drugs, opium, or LSD, your wisdom and judgment become torpid, and you are intoxicated. Your wisdom is gone and you are intoxicated. When you take these (drugs), you see the dance of illusion. When you take these, you see this, and you are mesmerized. These show you whatever you are thinking. If you take marijuana, you will see in a bewildered and confused way. That is how you will see. You will see what you are thinking. If you take marijuana, you will see in an illusory way. If you are laughing inside, you will see laughter outside. If you are crying inside, you will see crying outside. If you want a woman, you will see that. It will show you whatever you are thinking. Opium and chemical drugs, such as LSD, are like this. If you bring up your body by using these chemical drugs, what will you see? You will see the visions of your mind. You will see the thoughts of illusion and the visions of your mind.

However, when you look with wisdom at the truth, you will see God's kingdom. That is a Power. It has no form, shape, color, or hue. It is a very great Power. You can see that. The world is a tiny particle of dust, tinier than the point of a needle, but God's kingdom is very great. Know yourself. When you look within, you will find a kingdom, the kingdom of God. There is one point there, an atom. That is the kingdom of God. When you look at that kingdom of God with wisdom, when you look through the microscope of wisdom, you will see that it is a huge realm—it is a great thing. This world of the body will be destroyed, but the kingdom of God is permanent.

Think of this, he (the Shaikh) will say, and then he will show it to you. When he gives you the explanation, he will say: Earlier you were in the womb for ten months, were you not? You came from God, your Father. Did you understand the psychology that the psychology Doctor, God, your Father, taught you at that time? So many millions of diseases have come with you.

So many millions upon millions of diseases are connected to
you:

arrogance, karma, and maya,

tārahan, singhan, and *sūran,* the three sons of maya,

desire, anger, miserliness, attachment, fanaticism, and envy,

intoxicants, lust, theft, murder, and falsehood,

mind and desire,

maya, darkness,

so many thoughts;

all of these are diseases:

race, religion, scriptures, languages, color, hue,

the divisions and separations of "I and you," "mine and yours,"

earth, woman, and gold.

Like this, there are countless diseases with you now, and each
disease has an opposite. One is good and one is the opposite. Each
has something that is opposite to it. That opposite is also within
you. The opposite of right is *bad,* wrong. There is good and bad,
truth and falsehood, light and night, sun and moon, the pure soul
and the impure soul, the pure spirit and the impure spirit. The
good light life and the false life—the worldly life, the earth life, the
fire life. Like this, there are many opposites.

You can bend the sky into a bow. Viruses and cells can enter
you and travel from place to place. If you do this, are you a man?
No. For you to enter God and for God to enter you is the miracle.
Your wisdom must enter God and God's wisdom must enter you.
If you walk on fire, is that a miracle? Viruses can walk on fire. If
you walk on water, is that a miracle? Fish and viruses can also
walk on water. What does it matter if you rule the world? Everything, the reptiles and all the animals, birds, demons, and ghosts

consider this their kingdom. What is the use of your trying to rule the world? You need to rule the world within you. There is a huge world within you, a world of torpor, a world of illusion, a world of lack of wisdom, a world of ignorance, a world of false wisdom, and a world of scientific wisdom. You must control and rule this world with the world of true wisdom. You are a huge world and your body is a huge world. Within that there is truth, and with that power you should try to rule it. The Insān Kāmil, the Shaikh, will explain and show you this.

All right. Taking you along, he will say: Now look, this is the house you lived in earlier. Did you see it? It is made of earth, fire, water, air, and ether. The water changed into blood, the blood changed into milk, and you considered this section, this blood, as joy. It is blood. It is water that changed into blood. The blood changed into a blood clot, the blood clot changed into a piece of flesh, the piece of flesh rolled, whirled, and changed into the five elements, the five elements changed into the five letters, the five letters changed into this body, this body changed into this world, and this world shows the twelve causes, *kāranangal:*[2] the two eyes, two nostrils, two ears, the mouth, the two openings below, one, the navel, which has been cut and closed, (and the two openings above, the *kursī* and the *'arsh*). These are the twelve openings. Of these twelve openings, the seven above and the two below are the nine planets that make you agitated, *āddu.*[3]

The eyes make you agitated. The nose makes you agitated. There are good smells and bad smells, and there are good scenes and bad scenes; these make you agitated. There are good sounds and bad sounds; these make you agitated. There are good tastes

---

2. *kāranam, kāranangal* (plural) (T) Cause, basis, origin, source, principle, reason, means.

3. *āddu* (T) Agitate, shake, wave, move, dance, harass, trouble.

and bad tastes; these make you agitated. There is good speech and bad speech; these make you agitated. Sex and the arts and sciences are agitating you. The sixty-four sexual arts and the sixty-four arts and sciences are making you agitated. Fecal arrogance, *pē madam*,[4] is agitating you. Your food is arrogance, this is agitating you.

These are the nine planets, and they are making you agitated. You must conquer these planets. This is the house you lived in earlier. You built this house. Within it is the kingdom of hell and the kingdom of heaven, good and bad, the story of man-God and God-man, man-animal and animal-man, man-snake and snake-man. All these animals and qualities are within this world of your body. There are so many tens of millions of them. Do you understand this? Understand it.

This psychology is God's psychology. God created this; He knew, and He created these pairs of opposites. One is right, one is wrong. One is truth, one is falsehood. One is poison, one is good. One is right, one is wrong. One is good, one is bad. One is light, one is night. One is the sun, one is the moon. Understand this. He placed and created these opposites for you to know what is bad, to correct it, and to use it for what is good.

Water and fire are opposites. If you pour water on fire, the fire will be extinguished. Learn to use the fire in a good way. If you put fire under water, it will heat the water and become useful. Take the air. Do not throw the air away, but take the oxygen in the air and use it for a good purpose. Control the fecal arrogance of the elephant with what is good. Climb on that elephant, guide and control it, and make the elephant do work in the world, work

---

4. *pē madam* (T) Fecal arrogance; the place from which arrogance arises; arrogance arising from the fire of the anus.

which man cannot do. Control all the demons, ghosts, jinns, and fairies. Control the desires of your mind. Make them into something useful, train them to do what is beneficial. Do not use them for bad purposes, for what is opposite.

If you destroy the good and do what is bad, then that will destroy you. One is something that can destroy you; the other is something that can make you grow. You should control what is bad and make it work for you. If you let what is bad control you, that is your illness. You should understand this. To study and understand what can destroy you is the psychology of God.

(God says,) "I did all of this so you could understand. I am teaching you this so that you will understand it. I am teaching you this. Water became a blood clot, that became a piece of flesh, that became the five letters, and that became the five elements. From that you were made into a form, and this house was built. For ten months I taught you. Who is your relative? Who did you see there? Did you smell any fragrance there? You lived in this disgusting body of hell, this house of hell. Was there any fragrance there? No. Did you speak to anyone in this hell? No.

"You knew only Me, and I knew only you. The two of us were speaking with each other. Who was giving you milk? Who taught you and nurtured you? Who gave you eyes? Who placed the point within that? Who gave you a nose? Who placed the tiny point within the nose with which to smell? Who gave you ears and placed within them the tiny point which hears sound? Who gave you a tongue and placed within it a point which tastes? Who created speech? Who created the voice with which to make sound, and who is the One who placed the many different sounds within it? Who created your body? Who placed the *qalb* within that body? Who placed the point of truth within that *qalb*?

"Who placed these hands, legs, body, stomach, fire, for a reason, and who nurtured you and spoke to you? Did you see anyone else? Did you know the realm of hell you were in? Did you know you were formed from blood? No. The connection there was between you and Me. I spoke to you. For ten months in the womb, you and I were speaking. Whatever you asked for, I gave you. Whatever you said, I listened to. In this way, for ten months, you and I were alone. You and I were speaking with each other. You were praying to Me, and I was praising you. You were talking to Me, and I was doing your duty and your work. I was there, embracing you. You were embracing Me and I was embracing you. Both of us were embracing, is that not so? Did you not see this? This is the way we were together for ten months. Now what have you seen? Ah, *shari*,[5] understand this." (This is what God said.)

This connection must now be reconnected. Now you must connect again to the One who was connected to you and nurtured you in the womb, the One who spoke to you and taught you in the womb. For a while you forgot Him. This is what the Shaikh, the Insān Kāmil says. Now, this is the lesson you must learn. This is what we must study.

(God says,) "At that time you had nothing, no hell, heaven, kin, relationships, attachments, mother, race, religion, scriptures, language. You had none of these. Your language was Mine and My language was yours. We both spoke only one language—mystery, truth. That was the only language. You thought only of Me, I thought only of you. You spoke to Me, I spoke to you. You and I had one language of unity. You and I had one heart. That was our language. You and I had the same vision, you and I had the same food, you and I had the same body, you and I had the same action, you and I had the same duty, you and I had tranquility and

---

5. *shari* (T) All right, correct, good, okay.

peace together. You and I served with equality. We did duty with tranquility, peace, equanimity, and equality. There was nothing else. This was our language of unity. This is honesty; this is justice. We must act with the three thousand gracious qualities and the ninety-nine duties, *wilāyats*," God says.

This is what we must study. The Shaikh says: This is our language—unity, peace, and tranquility. This is our language; this is what God taught us previously. This is the language we learned for ten months. This is the language we learned when we were with Him. We must relearn this. This is the one language. This is unity. We must learn His language, and do that duty. *Sabūr,* inner patience, *shakūr,* contentment, *tawakkul,* trust in God, and *al-hamdu lillāh,* giving all praise to God—this is the preface (of *Īmān*-Islām). We must know these. Let us learn this lesson. This is what the Insān Kāmil, the Shaikh, says.

Now do you understand? God's psychology. This is what an Insān Kāmil does. Just as the child learned while he was an embryo, in that state he (the Insān Kāmil) starts to teach him again. He shows everything to him, and teaches him once again to speak to Him (God). It is in this state that an Insān Kāmil teaches each section.

In the same way a farmer plants seeds and trees and grows crops on the farm, and then brings the crops to maturity and makes them beneficial, an Insān Kāmil will raise us from the place that we are in, and, step by step, he will train us until we reach the right state. That is the book. He will change our qualities, and he will teach God's qualities, God's conduct, God's behavior, God's actions, God's love, and the truth. He will keep teaching, teaching, teaching, teaching—teaching that duty. That is how he trains us, by teaching these—that speech, that wisdom, that awareness, that perception, that intellect, that judgment, that subtle wisdom, that divine analytic wisdom, that *gnāna arivu,* divine wisdom, God's wisdom, *Nūr arivu,* the wisdom of Light, man-God, life, and the one Point.

He created both. He will show the point of one living in the other. When everything else is destroyed and one life emerges, then we will understand that God is within man and man is within God, God's kingdom is within man and man's kingdom is within God, God's story is within man and man's story is within God, God is man's secret and man is God's secret, God's property is man and man's property is God, the history of God is the history of man and the history of man is the history of God. This is a secret, this is a mystery. He shows that this is a mystery. He shows these and explains the kingdom of heaven and the kingdom of hell, man and man-animal, *insān-hayawān.* He gives the explanation of birth and of wisdom, and teaches about wisdom while on the path. The Shaikh embraces the child and explains to him while he is taking him along. The book is there. That is the book.

While traveling on the path, he shows the book. That is the explanation. One is wrong, one is right; you need this, you do not need that. This is a wonder, this is happiness, these are scenes, this is an example, this is a fundamental truth, this is good, this is bad. He will show each thing and explain it. An Insān Kāmil will embrace the child to his heart, and do his duty and keep showing him. To teach you from what you have kept within yourself, to teach you and show you with wisdom is psychology. There are no questions, there are no questions there.

God created you and the world, and He teaches you. He created you, He created the world, and He created all beings. He understands and teaches them, and He rules them. He is the One who knows and rules in this way. He is the One who is teaching. In the same way that God teaches and shows you, an Insān

Kāmil teaches you, using your body, using your sight, using your thoughts, using your intentions, using your mind and desire. He teaches you using your life and shows you both the wrong and the right. He teaches you both, using what you have already learned. Using your tongue, he shows you wrong and right. Using the food you eat, he teaches you what is wrong and right, and what is *halāl* and *harām*, permissible and impermissible. Using your thoughts, he shows you what is good and what is bad. He teaches you using what you have. He takes the book of your body and shows you the wrong and the right. From your thoughts, joy, sorrow, happiness, and sadness, from whatever happiness or sorrow you have, he will take that and show it to you.

This is how the Insān Kāmil teaches you from your body and from your own thoughts. Psychology, this is psychology. He takes and teaches you from what you have. He teaches you from your intentions. He gives the explanation from your thoughts. He gives the explanation from your heart, *qalb*. He teaches you from your mind, and he teaches you from your hands and feet. Like this, he teaches you from your own birth, from your life.

An Insān Kāmil uses psychology in the same way that God teaches His creations, by understanding each person. This is the psychology where he takes what is inside you, understands what is inside you, and teaches you. This is God's psychology. The Shaikh does not ask: What is happening to you, what is happening here, what is happening there? There is no room for questions like that. He takes your state and what is inside you, and teaches you from that. When you come before a Shaikh, what is revealed is what is already within you. It is revealed in the same way a mirror reflects back what is in front of it. What comes before the Shaikh, the true Insān Kāmil, is reflected back. No matter what you come with, he knows it. The Shaikh does not need to ask. He knows what is in

your mind, your qualities, and your actions. He can immediately
see that. That is psychology, God's psychology. Then he comforts;
he gives the explanation and gives peace.

This is not a miracle. What is a miracle? When you look at
yourself, at your body, and see God's Light within you, that is a
miracle. For your eyes to look at God and see God's secret won-
ders, that is a miracle. For your nose to smell the fragrance of
God's kingdom and Power, that is a miracle. For His Light to
resplend in your face like the full moon and for that beauty to
be seen in you, that is a miracle. When the peace of His kingdom
resplends in your heart and you are at peace and have tranquility
in your body, that is a miracle. When your hands and feet do His
duty and find complete satisfaction in that duty, that is a miracle.
If you can make the world die in you before you die, and if you
can receive a life for yourself in God's kingdom and be serene and
happy, that is a miracle.

This is the miracle that is within you. You do not have to show
this to others. It is not a miracle, a siddhi to be outwardly dis-
played. Making your life into God's life is a miracle. Making your
thought into God's thought is a miracle. Making your sight into
God's sight is a miracle. Making your speech into God's speech
is a miracle. Making your fragrance into the fragrance of God is
a miracle. Making your body into God's kingdom is a miracle.
Making your intentions and thoughts into God's intentions and
thoughts is a miracle.

This is rightfully yours, this is what you need to do. What
other miracle is there? Is it a miracle to fly in the sky, doing the
work of a bird or a honeybee? Is it a miracle to perform magic? It
is not a miracle. Is doing the work of a fish, walking on water, a
miracle? Is walking on fire like a virus, or bending the sky into a
bow, or doing tricks a miracle? It is not. Is it a miracle to do yoga,

standing on one leg for hours at a time like a stork does to catch a fish, or is it (a miracle) to hold the breath like the work a snake does?

You are a human being. Do not do the work of an animal. Do not do the boxing work of a monkey or a kangaroo. Can you gain a title from this? Do you want to do the work of an elephant and appear strong and lift up a car? That is the work an elephant does. You are unable to carry the world, and you are struggling. You do not have the strength to brush aside this world that is just a tiny point, but you are trying so hard to carry a house, like an elephant. You are unable to carry your small mind. You are struggling so hard and have no strength or tranquility. This is what you must conquer so you can find peace.

This is what the Insān Kāmil explains to you. These are the explanations he gives you. False wisdom, ignorance, science, and true wisdom are within you. These are inside you. God's kingdom and plenitude are also within you. You must learn about these. Everything can be learned within your body. All the examples and fundamental principles that are within you must be examined.

An Insān Kāmil is the truth. He is the only human being in this world. It is very rare and difficult to find him. It is not easy to find him. Like the bat that goes in search of fruit, you should search for him with wisdom, and find him. Then you can have peace and realize tranquility. Only then will you find peace.

My love you. We will speak later. Now we will stop.

A'ūdhu billāhi minash-shaitānir-rajīm.
I seek refuge in God from the accursed satan.

Bismillāhir-Rahmānir-Rahīm.
In the name of God, the Most Compassionate, the Most Merciful.

Drop Your Burdens and Proceed

March 11, 1982, Thursday 6:15 AM

M. R. Bawa Muhaiyaddeen ☺ addresses a disciple.

A worm lives in a particular place. If the worm goes to another place, it might cause harm to someone. If rice is put into a hellish place, it becomes harmful and cannot be eaten. Like this, you should analyze and understand the meaning of my every word.

Pullai, child, sometimes, while I am discoursing, your mind becomes confused, and you start crying. You cry about everything. However, everything I am showing you, all of the examples given, are explanations to correct you, to show you the way the world is or the way something else is.

When there is a movie, a story, a word, a hadith, or a speech, you worry. You do not take in the explanation, the essence, the wisdom, the truth, or the point. When you watch a movie, you say, "Ohh, oh oh, *aiyō,* they are doing this! Now they are doing that!" This is what you do when you watch a movie, or when you look at food, at insects, at demons, at satan, or at the nature of the world.

The good people will be made to suffer.
The evil people will be praised.

(In this world,) the good people will be made to suffer, and the evil people will be praised. Those who speak treacherous and deceitful words will be considered great. Treachery will rule. The tricks of deceitful people will rule the world. The good people will be made to suffer and the bad people will be praised. This is the world. It will be ruled by deceitful words; it will be ruled by cheating and treachery. This state will come to the world.

There is good and evil, wisdom and ignorance, truth and falsehood. This is a different learning from that.

Creation is the foundation, *ātāram*.

Within creation exist cause and effect, *kāranam* and *kāriyam*.

The created world is an example.

Creations are the cause.

Learning is the effect.

Understanding is the effect.

If you understand this, within that will be the Truth.

That Truth is God.

God is Wisdom.

God exists as the Wise One.

Without understanding this, you look at everything that happens, and either you cry or you worry or you run away, or you get sad or dejected. This is what you have learned. You do this. When you entered this room, something might have been happening here. I might have had some other work, I might have had some other concern. I might have been talking to someone else. I might have been ill. I might have been sleeping. I might have been speaking. I might have been answering someone's questions, or

I might have been looking into some other matter. You should not say, "When I came in, he didn't speak to me. He didn't notice me." You should consider the state of what is happening.

He[1] might not have been in this cage (body) at that time, he might have been in another cage. He might have been working in another house, he was not in this house at that time. Only when he returns to this house can he give you attention. You looked incorrectly with your wisdom—at that time he had changed houses; he had gone somewhere else. Only when he returns to this house where he is raising his child can he see you. Only if he comes back to this house can he look at you. He had gone to another house for another job. You were not in that house when he was doing that work, you are in this house. Only when he returns to the house where you are can he attend to you. Only when he has finished that work can he do this. Then he will inquire, "Where are my children? Where is that child? Did she eat? Where did she go?"

You must change your qualities and actions, and use your wisdom. You must establish truth in your *qalb;* then you will understand. This (behavior) is just like a baby's, the quality of a small baby who cries, "I want to go to the market. I want to go here and there. You didn't buy this for me. You didn't give me that, oooh." This is like a baby, "You didn't look after me. You didn't give me anything. This is not fair." This is the way it is.

A Father has to do many different jobs and visit many different houses. Sometimes he has to change houses, he has to go to another house. But you are not there. He has to go to another house and finish the work in that house; he has to look after the children who are there. Then he goes to a different house and does

---

1. In this section of the discourse, Bawa Muhaiyaddeen ☺ fluctuates between addressing himself as "I" and "he."

the work there, he looks after the children there. Then he goes to
another house where there are babies who need milk. He arrives
at the time the milk is needed and when that work is finished, he
remembers and returns here. Once he returns, he asks, "Where is
that child? Did that child eat? Where did that child go?"

You are acting like a baby. All your suffering is caused by your
own faults, your own doubt and suspicion, and your own anger.
This is the ignorance and lack of wisdom you are nurturing. What
can I say? I have been telling you this for many days, but it has not
penetrated. Sometimes when I sit here someone gives me water,
but I do not know I am drinking the water, and so I ask again,
"Please give me some water." I do not remember having taken the
water. I am not aware that the water actually went inside my body.
When I am speaking, I am unaware of what I am doing. When I
am immersed in a point, I do not know anything else. I may have
started something earlier and said to put it aside, but I will not
remember it until later. I am not aware of it. You might have seen
this sometimes. When I am working, someone may stand here
with some water. I might take it and drink it, but then I might not
remember that I drank it. When I have finished speaking, I ask,
"Didn't you give me any water?" And they will say, "We did give
you some water." Then I will ask, "Ah, is that so? Did I drink the
water?" This is how my life is. Sometimes I am unaware of what
you give me. Sometimes I am unaware of the work you are doing,
so when you come, I will ask you about it.

Give up this ignorance. Learn wisdom, learn love. That will
be good. Then you can be without sorrow. As long as you have
ignorance and lack of wisdom, you will suffer. If you cannot find
peace here, you will not find peace anywhere else in the world. If
you have not learned love here, you will not learn love anywhere
else in the world. If you have not improved your life here, you will

not improve your life anywhere else in the world. If you have not found the way to make the connection to God here, you will not be able to find this connection anywhere else in the world. If you have not found the truth here, you will not be able to find it anywhere else in the world, no matter where you go in this world. If you have not found equality and peace in your life here, you will not find it, no matter where else you go. If you have not found the explanation, the wisdom, and the subtle way to God, man, and duty here, you will not find it anywhere else in your life. You will not find it anywhere else, and your life will be one of sorrow. Only if you find this point here will you find peace and equality in your life.

If I touch you, there will be a reason. I would not touch you without a particular reason. The reason is a secret. You may have an illness, or an illness may be coming to you, or it may be that something is going to happen to you later, or a cyst may be forming, or some kind of cancer is coming, or something is going to happen to your nose, or to your head, or to your body. There is a reason this hand touches you. If some kind of karma is coming, then my hand touches you to release you from that karma. There is a reason my hand touches you; otherwise I would not touch you. When you have that wisdom and reach a place of understanding, you will realize, "This was the reason. It was to prevent some kind of illness from coming to me. This was the reason for the touch." Later, when you have wisdom and the illness begins to disappear, you will understand the reason for it. You should think of this. Right now you cannot understand this. What was going to happen later has been prevented at an earlier time.

Ah *shari*, all right. What can I do? I can only give you the drink that is needed. If a child refuses to drink, how can I make him drink? I rock the child, cradle him, and embrace him to my chest. I try to feed him. I hold him in my lap, hug him to my breast, hold him with my hands, and try to feed him. But if, in his ignorance and lack of wisdom, the child keeps pushing (the food) away, what can I do? Whether he is lying down or sitting, I try to feed him. Some children push the food away, some children are like this. If there is hastiness and impatience in everything one does—in one's wisdom, in one's work, in one's words, in one's actions, and in one's speech—if one acts with the mind, that is not good.

To take water from a river, you need a pot. You must take the water in something that will contain it. If you do not have a vessel that will hold the water, you cannot take it; the water will flow out. Similarly, it is with a quality that you must try to take a quality. With patience you must try to take patience. Only then can you take it. With good thoughts, try to take good thoughts. With that thought, try to take a deeper thought. With good qualities take better qualities. With patience take deeper patience. Wisdom must take deeper wisdom. God has to take God; with truth and peace you must take God deeply within. The vessel does not contain the water, but using that vessel you must draw in the water so you can drink and be peaceful. Fire can only be taken by fire. Therefore, you must use a pot that can bear the heat of the fire. This is the way you must learn wisdom. Your ignorance, your impatience, hastiness, and lack of wisdom are your illness.

Some children have suffered a great deal in their lives. Even before you finished school and went to work, you suffered a lot in your life due to ignorance, or your friends, or your relations, or your mother and father, or because of your husband, or your job or school or studies. Certain things caused this. That opposite is an illness. Because of that illness you developed hatred, and you have been leading your life with that hatred, without understanding the explanation—hatred because of your husband or children or life or the university or your friends.

You have been living your life according to the big things that happened to you earlier. That section may have occurred either artificially or naturally, but you still have it on your mind. You have not been able to throw it away, you are still unable to remove it. Because you cannot put it down, you are suffering—you have hastiness, impatience, and anger. Some children are mistreated by their parents, some children are mistreated by their mother. You have experienced these difficulties at various stages of your life. These difficulties may have been acquired or natural, but you are clinging to the memories. You are keeping these with you, and because of this, you are suffering in your life. You have not put them down. If you can put them down, you might change. If you do not put them down, you will continue to suffer.

This state is still with you. Instead of learning and gaining understanding from your experience, you carry around the memory of it. Some people are like this, *many* people are like this. What is the use of all your studying if you do not understand what real learning is? You do not understand that learning, and this is the cause of your suffering.

This is why you need a Shaikh, a Father, an *ānmā Tahappan*—a Father of the soul. He will look at your state, and he will look at your mind. He will look at each section in order to make you grow, to make your soul grow.

All these days the world brought you up. Science, *vingnānam*, brought you up. Ignorance, *agnānam*, brought you up. False wisdom, *poygnānam*, brought you up. But when you come to a Father, an Insān Kāmil, he will develop the true wisdom, *meygnānam*, of your soul.

Different things exist in the world: false wisdom, ignorance, and science. False wisdom, *poygnānam,* always exists naturally in the world, in darkness. There is no understanding within it; it is just there as an ordinary thing.

Ignorance, *agnānam,* decorates false wisdom and makes it beautiful. It makes it attractive, puts on makeup, builds a house, paints it, constructs a door, and creates air flow. It makes the body, clothing, and food a little clearer and more beautiful.

Science, *vingnānam,* invents things with instruments, with the atom, with air, with fire, with water, and with earth. Using intellect, it decorates. It develops more important facts and decorates them further. It takes knowledge, books, and lettering and makes them even more beautiful, using the tools of the five elements, the five letters.

The body is made of the same five letters. What you are experiencing and enjoying is also the same five letters, earth, fire, water, air, (and ether), the five letters of the body. Those five letters started as false wisdom, as creation. Then they became more beautiful and developed into ignorance. Then, with those five letters, science was developed, making the world more attractive and inventing various instruments and other things.

This is the body. Within this body there is another body. To reveal the body's basic nature you need an Insān Kāmil. What brings out its (the other body's) beauty, and what explains its meaning and essence is *meygnānam,* true wisdom. His (the Insān Kāmil's) work is to raise you with that wisdom and with truth.

There is another form. As the child grows, he (the Insān Kāmil) tries to help develop that form. Having developed it, he will bring you to the *Nūr,* the Light, which is Plenitude—to the Truth, God, that Power, *gnānam,* the complete wisdom. That Plenitude is God. He will bring you up so that you can learn complete wisdom, so you can reach that Perfection. That is an Insān Kāmil.

To bring you to that state, he will separate you from the two sections of creation and the world that you knew and experienced earlier as truth and goodness. He will show you all this. This is not in a book. You are still holding onto the book that you learned from in your life. You are holding onto what you perceived as joy and sorrow and as truth and falsehood, are you not? You have learned that this was happiness, this was sorrow, this was truth, and this was life. You learned it before, did you not? You have held onto that world. That is the world of creation, the world of the sexual games, the sixty-four arts and sciences, and ignorance. You researched into all of these and acted on them. This is science. You learned from books; you learned this, and you considered it to be true.

You have kept that book, the book of your birth that shows you what you saw as true and what you saw as false. He (the Insān Kāmil) takes this book that you have, and shows it to you. He also shows you the book that he has, the book of *meygnānam,* true wisdom. He reveals the meanings of both.

He shows you from what you see. He explains:

This is this. This is that.
This is the world. That is the world of God.
This is the life of the world. That is the life of God.
This is the life of ignorance. That is the life of wisdom.
This is the life of the impure spirits. That is the life of
the pure spirit.

This is the life of truth. That is the life of falsehood.
This is the life of duty. That is the life of the energy of
self-business.

This is the life without attachment. That is the life
of attachment.
This duty is done without attachment. That duty is done
with attachment.
This is a life of compassion. That is a life with blood attachment.
This is God's quality. That is the quality of blood ties.
This is fascination, *mayakkam*, with truth and God. That is
fascination with the world of illusion.
This is God's vision. That is the vision of the world, your vision.
This is God's duty and qualities. Those are the qualities
of illusion, of the body of five elements.
This is God's heart or *qalb*. That is the monkey mind of illusion.
This is God's wish, *āsai*, His equality, the desire for peace
and tranquility.
That is the desire of the dog whose tongue continuously
hangs out, panting and licking the world.
This is God's love and happiness. That is the sexual joy of the
body of the five elements of illusion and the sensual pleasures.
This is God's path. That is the path of fecal arrogance.
This is God's religion, the religion of truth, *sattiya vēdam*,
of one family and one scripture. That is the religion that
contains divisions, fighting, separations, and differences.
This is the one learning. That is a learning which contains
everything that the mind has gathered from the world,
and which causes accidents.
This is the *beauty form*, the one beauty of God's family,
God's beauty, God's speech, God's gaze, God's thoughts,
actions, and qualities. That is the earth, fire, water, air, ether,
mind, desire, and the four hundred trillion, ten thousand
spiritual qualities and thoughts.

Suffering is natural to your life. Happiness is also natural
to your life.
Whatever you learn in life, whatever you take from it,
and whatever you do in it causes you suffering.
The Insān Kāmil will explain this.

Like this, the Insān Kāmil will show you these two sections.
Feeding you the milk of wisdom, God's love, and God's compassion, he will bring you to wherever you have to be brought. He
will explain and show each thing from the book that you have
kept and read. He will take your qualities and show you. He will
take your actions and show you. He will show you from the way
you sleep, the way you sit, the way you act, the way you dress, the
way you look, the way you think, the way you eat, and the way you
drink. From whatever you have within you, he will show you.

You must give up these qualities and change to the quality of a
baby. That baby is the baby of *gnānam,* divine wisdom, which the
Insān Kāmil raises. If you change into that, you become a baby
of *gnānam.* But, if you continue to hold onto and roll around in
the book that you are keeping with you, then that is the section of
hell. That is the section of the hell of birth. His work is to change
each quality that you have, to change each of your actions, and to
make you into a small child—to change you into a baby of *gnānam,* God's child. Only if you give up what you had earlier can you
change into God's baby. You must keep changing and become
a baby of *gnānam,* God's baby. You must change into His child,
become that baby. That is his (the Insān Kāmil's) work. As long as
you do not put down all the burdens and change the qualities that
you have, you are the world; you are this world of hell.

There is a huge world within you, within your body. Your
mind is a huge world of illusion. You yourself are a huge book.

Everything you have learned is a book; everything you have seen is a book; everything you have understood is a book. Everything you have ever done are your experiences, joys, and sorrows. But if you change and come to a really good place and then look back, you will see that everything is false. All that you saw as true is false. All that you saw as good is evil. All that you thought was attachment is sin. All those you considered as relations are tigers and lions. All those you considered as friends are poisonous beings. All those you considered as loved ones are demons that will eat you and drink your blood. You need to understand this.

Only when you have changed and looked back will you see this. You will not know this until your attachments change, until you change from the kingdom of the world to the kingdom of God. Until then, you will think that what you see is real. You will think that the tastes, the food, the speech, the learning, and the actions you have experienced are real. But when you change, section by section, and then look back, you will understand that it is because of each of these that sorrow came to you. Every learning is like this. Every gaze is like this. Every thought is like this. Every action is like this. Every conduct is like this. Every quality is like this. Every behavior is like this. Every love is like this. Every kindness is like this. Once you change, you will know which beings are eating you. If you change and look back, you will see which are consuming you. If you change and look back, you will see those evil qualities, and realize, "Ohhh, those are the things that were eating me. It was because of ignorance that I held onto those things." As long as you do not change, all the suffering you have kept with you will consume you.

An Insān Kāmil, a Father, will change this. As long as you do not change into a baby, as long as you do not change into a baby of *gnānam,* as long as you do not change into a baby of wisdom, as long as you do not change into a child of God, you will only have the things that you have kept with you—earth, fire, water, air, ether, mind, and desire and the four hundred trillion, ten thousand thoughts. Everything you collected in this section of hell, everything you gathered and saw as happiness is eating you. This is what is killing you. Think of this.

This is psychology:
to understand the freedom of your soul and to understand
the world,
to understand your cage and the country,
to understand yourself and others,
to understand the pure soul and the impure soul,
to understand the kingdom of heaven and the kingdom of hell,
to understand God and illusion,
to understand truth and satan,
to understand light and darkness,
to understand good qualities and bad qualities,
to understand good actions and bad actions,
to understand patience and jealousy,
to understand *sabūr*, inner patience, and impatience
and hastiness,
to understand *shakūr*, contentment, which is God's quality,
and the arrogance of "I, I,"
to understand equality and what is called the "I,"
and to understand peace and the agitation of the mind.

You must understand each of these sections. You must understand the explanation of God's qualities and the qualities of the world, illusion, mind, and the five elements. The explanations are revealed within you, in your body, in the sky, in the earth, in the trees, in the bushes, in food, in sight, in thoughts, in the weeds, in the grass, inside and outside, in your learning, in sleep and in wakefulness, in your attachments, in your children, in your birth and in your death. These explanations are taken from within you and revealed to you. The reasons are shown according to these explanations: This is truth, that is falsehood; this is perishable, that is imperishable; this is true wisdom, that is ignorant wisdom; this is God's wisdom, that is the wisdom of satan's torpor; this is the wisdom of *gnānam,* that is the wisdom of ignorance. He will show each of these: This is God's quality, that is the quality of illusion, torpor, and satan; this is tranquility, that is the quality of the monkey mind; this is peace, that is your fire; this is unity, that is selfishness. You are shown this in yourself, in your cage (body), and in everything. You are made to know it; you are taught this.

The Insān Kāmil will teach this baby of God to be the leader in the kingdom of God and in the kingdom of the world, to control this (world) and to rule the kingdom of God. He will change you into his child, and in that state will comfort your life and give you peace. He is the *Ānmā Gnāni;*[2] he is the Insān Kāmil, the *Ānmā Gnāni* who reveals and explains purity and plenitude. He is the Insān Kāmil. This is what he does. This is his duty and his service, and through this he teaches: This is science and this is true wisdom. This is psychology, the learning within yourself. Without your asking, he gives you the explanation. What you do not realize, he makes you realize. You should reflect on this.

Beyond this, he shows the connection between you and God. He shows and explains the wisdom within wisdom. First he gives you the explanation through the six wisdoms, and when you have

---

2. *Ānmā Gnāni* (T) *Ānmā:* Soul, spirit, life. *Gnāni:* A man of wisdom.

reached that state (of understanding), he gives the explanation through *pērarivu*,[3] divine luminous wisdom, the explanation of God. He gives that explanation so that you can transcend the seven realms of the *dēva rāchiyam*, the kingdom of God, the seven heavens. Then he gives you the explanation of the secrets of the eighth heaven. That is the *ānmā rāchiyam*, the kingdom of the soul. He gives the explanation about that kingdom which is God's kingdom, the eighth heaven. That comes after you have learned about the other seven realms. Only when you have understood these can you understand (the eighth). Later, he will give that explanation of God's kingdom. First you have to change and grow. You must first understand these. He will show you what is necessary so that you can understand this. You should think about this.

This is the path that you, all of the children, and everyone must follow. This is the psychology of the true Insān Kāmil. He will not follow you; you must follow him. He will not go behind you. If you take your mind with you, you cannot go behind him. As you are following him, he will keep on revealing things to you. He will show you through words of wisdom; he will show you through examples; he will show you through what is good. He will show you the difference between the opposites of good and bad in your life: This is good, and that is bad. This is a quality, and that is a resulting action. You must look in a subtle way and understand it.

To mend a small tear you must first carefully draw the thread through the tiny eye of a needle. Then, as you are sewing, you must watch carefully, so as not to prick your finger. You need to

---

3. *pērarivu* (T) Divine luminous wisdom; the seventh of the seven levels of wisdom. This wisdom is the resplendent Light of Allāh, the wisdom of the *Nūr*.

pay attention as you put the needle into the cloth and pull it to the other side. You could be pricked on either side of the cloth, so you have to watch carefully. You have to watch where you put the needle in and where you pull it out.

Our life is torn like this. Our life has a huge rip in it. To mend it, we must put the thread of faith, of *īmān*, through the needle of intellect, and mend our life with that sharp point of wisdom. You must concentrate intently as you sew; otherwise you will be pricked, the tear will not be mended, and your hand will be pierced. If you prick your hand, you will be in trouble.

Like that, when the Insān Kāmil is teaching you, you must watch with vigilance, with great care, with *īmān*, and with determination. If you do not do this, it will prick you, it will hurt you. If you look here and there, it will be your fault.[4] Please think of this.

After this, with divine luminous wisdom, *pērarivu*, he will teach you how to cut divine luminous wisdom, and understand it. Having come to that state, he will show you how, with plenitude, to cut plenitude and merge as one with it. This is psychology. We will speak of this later.

You must know this, my children. You are the ones who are playing. You are the ones who pour sand over your own heads, and when it gets in your eyes, you are the ones who cry. So, what can we do? You take the fire, you play with it, you light the fire, and you burn yourself. It is not the fault of the fire, and it is not the fault of the earth. They are just (outer) causes. You take a knife, you play with it, and you cut yourself. You cut others and you cut yourself. Then you cry. In this way, everything you pick

---

4. *kutru* (T) Prick, puncture, pierce; *kutram* (T) Fault, blemish, defect. Bawa Muhaiyaddeen ☺ is punning on these two words.

up and play with becomes a weapon, and you cause suffering to others. These are the weapons you use.

The work of an Insān Kāmil is to show you how to make use of these so that they will not cause suffering to others, to show you the wrong and the right, to show you what each thing will do and how to handle it. He will explain about everything that you pick up. He will give you *proof:* This is what this will do, this is how it should be handled, this is how you should understand it. That is the work of an Insān Kāmil, a Father. But if you are not careful and do not follow what he says, you will be cut. You need to think of this.

Thank you. You need to understand this. There is no use crying about it. It is your ignorance and lack of wisdom that make you cry. Every child should think of this. You cry at least three or four times a week. I am not making you cry. You are the one crying. You are making yourself cry. Give this up. If you give up this section, you will not need to cry.

Since you came here you have been crying, child, *pullai.* You are nearly forty years old, and from the time you were twenty or twenty-one, you have been crying. You have been crying for the last nineteen or twenty years. Wherever you go, you cry. You cry in your life, you cry in school, you cry with your friends, you cry with your family, you cry at work, you cry when you go to buy a house, you cry when you go to your job. When is this going to end? Have you not asked yourself, "Why am I crying? What is the reason for my crying?" If only you would ask yourself that question, the crying would stop. There is no reason to cry. You should think, "I am crying because of an attachment I have. It is because of that connection that I am crying. I am weeping because of an attachment of the mind. If I can cut this attachment and discard it, I will not need to cry." You should think, "Twenty years have gone by, and there is no reason for me to cry now. I am going on my journey, and whatever loads I collected along the way, I must drop off at the different stations." Then, whatever a person gives you, you drop it off at its station. Everyone will give you something. If a friend gives you something, drop it somewhere and proceed.

A friend came and gave you a burden. Leave it there and proceed. Later, the parents gave you a burden. That is very difficult to carry. Put it down. Later a husband came and gave you some burdens. Put them down. In this way, drop the burden at each station and proceed. If you carry it with you on your journey, it will be difficult. Only carry one thing. Leave everything else behind. Then you will not cry. Why are you carrying the bundles you collected when you were studying, the bundles you collected from your learning, the bundles you collected when you were working, the bundles you collected from attachments, the bundles you collected from friends, the bundles you collected from your actions, the bundles you collected in life? Why are you carrying all of these burdens? Drop them at each station and proceed empty-handed and free. Board where you must board, and get off where you must get off. Instead of carrying burdens in your hands, on your nose, or on your head, just proceed on your journey. Then it will be easy.

At each moment, do what needs to be done. You will receive what you need for that moment. What is needed at a particular time will happen. That is His work. Proceed.

Continue on your journey, saying,
"I am doing the work You gave me now.
What I will do in the next moment is in Your *tawakkul,*
in Your responsibility.

I am asking forgiveness for whatever I did in the past
and for whatever I received in the past.
Astaghfirullāhal-'aliyyal-'azīm,
I ask Allāh, the Exalted and Supreme, for forgiveness.

"For whatever sins I committed,
astaghfirullāhal-'aliyyal-'azīm.

"What I am doing now is reciting (the *subhānallāhi kalimah*):

Subhānallāhi
wal-hamdu lillāhi
wa lā ilāha illAllāhu
wallāhu akbar
wa lā haula
wa lā quwwata
illā billāhi
wa huwal-'aliyyul-'azīm.

All glory is to Allāh
and all praise be to Allāh
and there is none worthy of worship other than You:
You are Allāh,
and Allāh is most great!
And there is no majesty or power
except with Allāh,
and He is most exalted, supreme in glory!

"This is to make my heart clear and to cut away karma.

Now I have to make my *qalb halāl*, permissible, with the
subhānallāhi kalimah."

Recite: "*Astaghfirullāhal-'aliyyal-'azīm.*
Please forgive me for all the sins I have committed."
Then recite the *tasbīh*, the *subhānallāhi kalimah*,
to cut away jealousy and ignorance from your *qalb*.

Do *qurbān*, the sacrifice of the *qalb*.
Sacrifice the *qalb*, perform *qurbān*.

This is what you should do for this time, for this *waqt*.

Do *tasbīh*, praising God. Do *tasbīh* to Āndavan, to God. Do
qurbān, sacrifice your *qalb*. Cut blood ties, ignorance, false wisdom, selfishness, jealousy, envy, vengeance, treachery, deceit, birth,
death, maya, darkness, torpor, and satan. Cut the qualities of the
dog, the donkey, the horse, the snake, the rat, revenge, and anger.

Cut all these with the *subhānallāhi kalimah*:

Subhānallāhi
wal-hamdu lillāhi
wa lā ilāha illAllāhu
wallāhu akbar
wa lā haula
wa lā quwwata
illā billāhi
wa huwal-'aliyyul-'azīm.

Saying this, perform *qurbān* on your *qalb*.

Ask for forgiveness for the sins you have committed, saying,

"*Astaghfirullāhal-'aliyyal-'azīm.*

I ask Allāh, the Exalted and Supreme, for forgiveness.

IllAllāh, You are Allāh." For what is to happen in the next *waqt*,

place your trust in Allāh, *tawakkulun 'alAllāh.*

If you continue your journey doing this, asking forgiveness, *taubah,* for what is past, and performing *qurbān* on the heart for the present; if you clear your *qalb* and give it to Allāh, handing over all responsibility to Him, and praising Him, *tasbīh,* if you do the duty of your journey of life, if you do the duty of the present moment, and if for the next *waqt* you have *tawakkul,* and surrender to Allāh, if you praise Him, *tasbīh,* and ask forgiveness, *taubah,* for what has happened—if you can go on your journey in this way, then your journey will be an easy one. Then you will be clear. Learn from the Shaikh, the wisdom and research that are necessary for this. Then your journey will be easy. Complete the work that is necessary for each moment.

As long as you do not reach this state, you will be the one crying and you will be the one laughing. You will be the one who is sad and you will be the one who is happy. Sorrow and joy will swing back and forth. Both wisdom and ignorance will be present, and you will have spoiled yourself. If you are suffering because of your own actions, what can be done? What can the Shaikh do, what can a wise man do? What can an Insān Kāmil, a physician of the soul, do? If one is suffering because of one's own actions, what can be done? What can the physician of the soul do? If you have ruined yourself, if you have spoiled yourself by grabbing onto everything, what can he do?

Stop causing suffering to yourself! Then the medicine of the physician of the soul will be acceptable to you, and his wisdom will work for you. Then you can gain freedom and peace. You will find peace within yourself, you will find equality within yourself, you will find tranquility within yourself, you will find impartiality within yourself. Then you will find the freedom of your soul, and you will understand the explanation of wisdom and the resonance of *gnānam*.

After that, you will know the kingdom of God, and in that state, you will change into God's child. Only when you change into God's child can you become a leader in the kingdom of God. Then you can receive that position; you can have that beauty and wear that crown. You can wear that crown. You can be a representative of His kingdom, and you can help all lives. You will be one who protects and comforts all lives. Otherwise, you will be the cause of your own crying.

It is not his fault. It is not the fault of the physician of the soul, it is not the fault of God who is the Physician within the physician. It is not the fault of the Insān Kāmil, and it is not the fault of Allāhu, who is the Kāmil within that kāmil, the Perfect within that perfected man.

Please reflect on this. *Āmīn*. So be it. *As-salāmu 'alaikum wa rahmatullāhi wa barakātahu kulluhu*. May all the peace, the beneficence, and the blessings of God be upon you.

Later I will give certain explanations. Everyone should please think about this.

A'ūdhu billāhi minash-shaitānir-rajīm.
I seek refuge in God from the accursed satan.

Bismillāhir-Rahmānir-Rahīm.
In the name of God, the Most Compassionate, the Most Merciful.

⚜ 8 ⚜

Communaisam and Communism: Love and Hate

March 12, 1982, Friday 7:00 AM

We are going to talk a little about the psychology of man's life. The state of man's life and his understanding of how to conduct his life will cause either his destruction or his growth. For growth, there is God's unity, God's qualities, peace, and tranquility. For destruction, there are the emotions of the mind and the emotions arising from the five elements of the body of illusion.

These two sections and two qualities do two kinds of work. One is the section of God—wisdom, integrity, unity, and peace. The other is the section of the world—illusion, mind and desire, satan, the selfish attachments to the body, and torpor. There are two sides, two forms, two qualities, and two sections. The life that one leads with a worldly foundation is a life of self-business.

A machine needs oil, gas, air, current, fire, and water. For it to work, it needs this section. This earth-body also needs these to move. Whatever is needed by a machine is also needed by the body.

There is another section, another quality: truth, unity, love, mercy, equality, peace, compassion, charity, and serenity—*communaisam,*[1] God's peace. Communaisam is to show equality to all

---

1. communaisam (E & T) Bawa Muhaiyaddeen ☺ combines the English word "common" with the Tamil word for love, "*naisam,*" to form the word communaisam—common or equal love for all.

111

lives, to love all lives as our own, to consider the sorrows of others as our own, to be without separation and differences, to consider the suffering of others as our suffering, the happiness of others as our happiness, the hunger of others as our hunger, and the illness of others as our illness.

Like this, there are God's three thousand gracious qualities and ninety-nine *wilāyats*, powers, and His actions, conduct, and behavior. These are the qualities of communaisam, the quality of loving and trusting all lives as one's own life, and protecting them, without separation. This is God's form; these qualities are God's Light form. If you take this form and analyze with it, you will realize the kingdom of God, His form and qualities. It is a kingdom of justice, a life of justice, a light form of justice, and a life of compassion. This is the way that form acts. It has no differences or separations. This is God's Light form. This is communaisam. Communaisam is to have love, *naisam*, for all of everything in the world—to have love and unity.

There is another quality. For a machine to run, it needs an engine, does it not? Like that, there are those who have attachment to their body and attachment to the world, who do self-business for their own gain, considering only their own hunger, their own comfort, their own house, their own money, their own property, their own business, their own life, their religion, their race, their scripture, their color, and their class. They think of themselves as great people, and this is the reason they live a life of selfishness. In this way, not thinking of others, they live their lives for themselves. With the selfishness of pride, arrogance, and karma, they make the kingdom and the land their own. They take what they want from the sixty-four arts and sciences and the sixty-four sexual games for their own gain.

Those who act in this way cause destruction. When that self-business grows, it separates into the three sections of arrogance, karma, and illusion. It separates into the three desires of desire for earth, desire for woman, and desire for gold. With these three desires, they conduct this section. Their life is to rule the earth, to control wealth, and to possess women. With wealth, earth, and the possession of women, they develop self-business in order to control the world.

Those who are in this state do not know communaisam. They have only the system of the emotions of their mind, the system of the emotions of illusion, mind and desire. It is with these that they conduct their lives. Some of them have titles, some are rich, some are rulers of the world, and some are great and famous in the world. In this life there are the poor, the rich, the famous, and the rulers. Every section of the poor people is crushed by the wealthy people. Because those who are wealthy do not have communaisam, because they have self-business, and because of their separations, they attack others. They attack the positions, wealth, and lives of others. They do this because they do not have love for other lives.

Ten out of a hundred people will reach a high status in these different sections. Ten out of a hundred will become successful in religion, ten out of a hundred will become successful in wealth, and ten out of a hundred will become successful in status. Seventy-five percent will be poor. The poor people also have an attachment to the world. When they have hunger, poverty, difficulty, famine, illness, and disease, and when they lose their houses and property, their qualities change. When their qualities and actions change, difficulties arise within the family and within their lives; there are difficulties and separations between the wife and husband, difficulties between the children and the father and mother, money problems, and job problems. Because of the hardships of poverty, the emotions of the mind are upset, and there is no unity in their lives. In that section, sorrow and separations increase and because of that the number of poor people increases. The powerful crush the poor, and the number of poor people increases.

Hatred changes those who are poor, and they will oppose race, religion, scripture, God, truth, and justice. They will ask, "What is this race? What is this religion? What is this scripture? What is this man? What is this God?" and will rebel against them. "What is this husband? What are these children? Everything is a lie." This is what they will say in their minds. When that unity, when that state of the section of the kingdom of God changes, those who are without that state change to this state.

Some people will become rich and some will become powerful, but those who become poor will come to this state. There will be poverty, difficulties, and joblessness in the country. A few people will have a great deal of wealth, while others will not even have a mat to sleep on or a house to live in or food to eat. As the powerful people keep crushing the life out of them, their state changes. Their psychological state changes, and that state changes their qualities. Their actions change to murder, theft, and lies. With the wrong state, they go on the wrong path, and then they do the work of prostitutes, thieves, and beggars. Even though they may have had honest qualities, their minds change; they change from the form they are in into another form, the form of an animal. As soon as they change, a system is formed. When that state comes, communism comes.

To go on God's path and to have God's qualities is communaisam. The other is communism—they start taking drugs, LSD, marijuana, opium, beer, brandy, and whisky. They take drugs and alcohol to induce a state of torpor so they can forget their suffering, and that causes a change in their emotions. When they take these intoxicants, it causes unrest and turmoil in their minds. These emotions cause the poor people to want to destroy the wealthy and powerful people who are causing them suffering. They say, "The people with status, the rich, and the religions must all be destroyed. We must all be equal." They do not understand God's qualities, the state of communaisam. They change into the other form, the form of the self-business of the world.

There are two forms. They change into this other form and are ruled by illusion, darkness, earth, fire, water, and air. On this destructive path, with these destructive qualities and this destructive form, they forget. They cut away the (good) section. They want to destroy the rich, those with wealth and status, and those who rule. Their minds change and their qualities change. As soon as their qualities change, the first thing they do is create poverty in the country. They kill all the rich people. They burn down any place there is money. They destroy the banks, burn up all the properties, and demolish everything in the city. They reduce to ruin everything that is contributing to the prosperity of the country, and create even more poverty.

Poisoning and murder come easy to someone who is suffering a great deal in his life. Both poisoning and murder become tasty to him and become his normal food. He eats the food of sin. Evil is tasty to him. He changes to that state, his mind changes to that state. These qualities change him to that state. Because of the cruelty of her husband, a wife might change. Because of what the father and mother did, a child might change to this state. Because of how the grandfather and grandmother are, others might change. Because of politics, the people might turn against the government. Because of the actions of a rich man, his servants and workers might turn against him. A wife might change because of what her husband did, and a husband might change because of what his wife did. The children might change because of what their mother and father did. This is how they change.

There are two sections. One is communaisam, God's section, which is the form of His qualities. The other is the quality of the five elements of the world, maya, the attachment of the body, and self-business. These are the two forms that man can change into. One side will form a system of destruction, and decide that the countries, the cities, as well as the evil people who are the cause of their suffering, must be destroyed. That is communism. Their first step is to destroy all the property of the rich people and all the businesses of religion. They will set fire to the rich people's houses and property, their means of transportation, the railways, and their banks. They will burn these and murder the people. The majority will do this. Next, they will bring poverty and difficulty to the people of that country, so that everyone descends to their state (of poverty). And those who are already poor will say, "What you said is true. This is good, this is right, now we are equal. Let everyone be like us!" When those who are poor hear people say that the rich should experience what they are experiencing, they say, "That's right. Oh, now we're equal."

This is the way this is created in the world. This is the way this second form is created. There is one form that is God's form, the Light form, the form of truth and justice. And there is another form, the form of the thoughts of the world of the five elements of earth, fire, water, air, (and ether), mind and desire, and the qualities of self-business, blood ties, maya, desire, and attachment. If this state comes, there will be destruction in the country. Religion will be destroyed, the wealthy will be destroyed, the rulers will be destroyed, unity and God's path will be destroyed, and God's communaisam will be destroyed. That communaisam will change to communism. Those qualities become communism.

When man changes into this state, that is communism.

These two different qualities are psychology. Man needs to understand this psychology. There are two sections, communaisam and communism. When this section grows, it is communism, and when that other section grows, it is communaisam. Communaisam will not hurt anyone; everyone is considered as equal to one's own life. Communism destroys everything that grows, and when that is finished, it is sealed, it is forever. It is permanent. When that is finished, there will be no more freedom. It will be the rule of the gun. The guns that were first used for destruction will later be used to control the people. That is forever. Just as the rich people were dictators, just as the wealthy gained power for their own self-gain, these people will become even more treacherous dictators with even more control. Their power will be the gun. No one will be allowed to speak. No one will be allowed to have an opinion. There will be no freedom. The gun will rule that kingdom; the gun becomes the dictator. This is communism.

The other is communaisam. Man needs to understand these two things. When communaisam grows in the correct way, man will have God's qualities, justice, and equality. He will consider the lives of others as his own life, the hunger of others as his own hunger, and the happiness of others as his own happiness. He will respect the freedom of others as his own. He will love everyone in the kingdom as he loves himself. In such a place, communism will not succeed, communaisam will grow. If God's justice is there, that (communism) will not grow.

Only if justice and (God's) qualities are destroyed in man can that (communism) grow. When that grows, it destroys God's qualities, justice, conscience, communaisam, religious worship, prayer, and peace. It will start with the rule of communism. When this happens, it will be the kingdom of the gun. The gun will rule that kingdom, and there will be no freedom after that. Their initial goals will not have been fulfilled. Only later will you realize that what they did has a very different point.

Both of these are psychology. When a man acts in this way, it is a disease, and when a man acts in that way, it is a disease. But if man understands the way to act, and if he comes to the correct state of communaisam, then he will not go on the wrong path of communism, and he will not be destroyed. If that justice, conscience, communaisam, and God's qualities and form grow in a man, he will not be destroyed. If love, *naisam*, is there, this system will not come.

Each man must understand this psychology within himself. He must understand his own life. Within himself, he must understand, "This is this quality. That is that quality. If this comes, this will happen. If not, that will happen." Both communaisam and communism exist in life. We must understand this about our lives. If *naisam* diminishes, if communaisam and God's qualities diminish, and if communism grows, then the state of separation and hatred will come. This will lead to a state where man will have no freedom in his life, and there will only be destruction.

Communism and destruction will flourish if communaisam diminishes in any country, kingdom, government, or society of man. Wherever there is wealth, the wealth will be destroyed by fire. This is the quality that is formed from hatred. Communism grows by creating hate in the country and then destroying the wealth. First they will create hardship and make the people join with them; then they will control them with force.

If communaisam: the wealth (of God), equality, peace, tranquility, conscience, and justice grows in man's society and country, then communism will not grow. In the state (of communism), there will be the separation of religion, separation of race, separation of color, separation of scripture, and separation of the "I" and "you." This is the point, the section that comes when people do business for self-gain, when they acquire status for themselves, and when they make wealth, earth, woman, and gold into their own kingdom. These qualities come. If man loses the qualities of communaisam and starts acting with self-business, then this is what comes next.

One is the form of communaisam and one is the form of communism. One is the form of destruction and one is communaisam, God's form and qualities. These two are within the life of man. Either one of these can come. If love, *naisam*, fails, this other will come. If justice wavers and self-business manifests, the other section will come. A man must be aware of this.

God's form, the form of truth, is Light. Man has two sections, two forms, and two qualities within him. One is the quality of destruction and one is the quality of peace. Both qualities are within man. If this grows, he will speak what is good; if that grows, he will speak what is evil and do what is evil. If this grows, he will do what is good; if that grows, he will do what is evil and have separations. If this grows, he will build a beautiful kingdom of justice; if that grows, he will build a kingdom of hell-fire and destruction. One shows the life of destruction and the other shows the life of peace, the life of God.

Man must be aware of these two sections. He must know them and study them. Both are within him—evil qualities and good qualities; equality and communaisam as well as self-business, destruction, and differences. If a man will understand both of these, if he will research into these two within himself, that is psychology. That state is the psychology of life.

God knows this. He has equality, peacefulness, and communaisam. Therefore, within His love, His *naisam*, there are no separations, religion, race, color, hue, or differences. There are no divisions. He is Love, *Naisam*, the Ruler of communaisam. His kingdom will never be destroyed. But if man divides His kingdom in two, if he discards God's kingdom and accepts the kingdom of hell, then he destroys himself. That kingdom of hell that he has accepted destroys his own life. He develops the instruments of his own destruction and places them in his own heart. He keeps those weapons of destruction within himself, and they destroy him. Every one of his qualities destroys him. Every thought and quality destroys him. These are the weapons. These are the weapons, the weapons of his life and his actions. The qualities and actions of his body and his thoughts are the weapons that destroy him, that destroy his world, his life, his body, and his heart. This is the world. In this world every thought is a bomb, every action is a bomb. Everything that he does with ignorance is a weapon that destroys this world of his life. This is the cause. This is what we must think about.

We must think of this and develop communaisam, the communaisam of the kingdom of heaven—justice, unity, peace, and the consideration of all lives equally. We must realize this peace in ourselves. When we give peace to all lives, that is the kingdom of heaven, the indestructible kingdom. That is a life that never perishes. That is the life of freedom and peace. We need to understand this.

My love you, my children. In this world there are two fundamental sections, *ātārangal*. One is communaisam, God's section; the other is communism, *our* system, the bad section. That system develops when we acquire these evil qualities, does it not? That is the system that develops. That system is the section of destruction. One man has two forms, two qualities. This form does the work that is good; that form does the work that is evil, it does the work of hatred, differences, jealousy, murder, and sin. In this state, man's mind, his intellect works in two sections. Both are in one body—these are beautiful qualities, those are evil qualities.

From these two bodies, we must control the one body. If we control those qualities, that body, and those thoughts, we will have peace. If we control this, we will have the section of good in our lives. If we can do this, we will always do what is good. We will realize peace and all lives will realize peace. Our lives will have unity. God and *we,* truth and *we,* justice and *we,* conscience and *we,* unity and *we,* equality and *we,* one race and *we,* one religion and *we,* one prayer and *we,* are together. This is psychology. One is the section of destruction, one is the section of progress. We should think of this.

My love you, my children, my sons, my daughters, my brothers and sisters, we should think about this. This is the research we need to understand. This is what we need to know. If we understand this and have justice within ourselves, we will have peace. If not, we will be in a state of differences, destruction, and separations. The religions must also research into this. The religions must think about unity, that there is only one God. The politicians need to think that there is only one justice, truth. The wealthy people must think that all lives are one life. Human beings must understand that we are all one family and that to create tranquility and peace, they must change to the good side of unity, God's side, the side of justice. Then, every life in this world will have peace; every life in every house, every person, every child, every wife, and every husband will realize peace in their lives. Then everyone will have peace and equality. This is what we must understand. Then there will be peace and tranquility in life. We need to think of this.

My love you. My God, Āndavan, may He teach us this knowledge. May He establish this state in us and give us wisdom and good qualities. May He give us clear wisdom to research and analyze ourselves. May He give us good qualities, peaceful qualities, tranquility, unity, and love, and may He protect us. May that Power, the God-Power, protect us. May we pray with our hearts that He will protect us.

Let us talk a little about Him, about psychology, the psychology of wisdom, about the psychology of clear wisdom. Let us talk further about the Power of God.

An example: When we build a machine, an engine, or a motor, what is needed for that machine to move is oil, gas, air, water, and fire. It is formed of metals from the earth. The different metals are melted and made into the machine. It needs water, oil, fire, gas, and air to start. What is the most important thing that it needs? What is necessary for that form, that body, to move? It needs water, oil, gas, air, and fire. Then it can move. Without these, the motor will not function. In order to make it work, it needs these.

Like this, man's body is a machine. This house is a "machine-house." This body that is made of earth needs water, oil, gas, and fire. Like this, it needs food, nourishment, and clothing. If we want to make use of it, these are necessary. Just as a machine requires certain things, man also needs those things. His body needs them.

If we do not give water to the machine that we built, if we do not take care of it, it will rust and become useless. It will be useless, that machine will be ruined. If we do not give it water, it will be ruined. Like this, we must give the body what it needs. A machine breaks down or burns out when it gets too little of what it needs. It will not start if there is not enough oil or not enough gas. It will explode if there is no air and no fire. If there is no water, it will explode and might hurt those who are near it.

Similarly, the body of man is like this. A man must be given the food and nourishment that is essential to his life; otherwise, it will be difficult. He will burst, his qualities will explode. The qualities in him will explode. His intellect will explode. His feeling, *unarvu,* awareness, *unarchi,* and intellect, *putti,* will explode. He will cause pain to others. This is the cause. He will not be of any benefit, and when he explodes, he will cause suffering to others. This machine is like this.

In this state, as soon as what is essential for man is reduced, when what is needed for that machine to work is reduced, when what is necessary to make the machine-body of man work is reduced, it will not function. But if what is necessary is given in the correct way, when water, air, and oil are correctly given, it will be able to keep on working.

When hunger comes, the ten will fly away, *pasi vandāl, pattum parandu poitch.*[2] The ten good qualities will fly away. When poverty comes, his qualities change. When difficulties come, he loses his faith. When suffering, illness, disease, sorrow, and worry come, he comes to the state where he loses everything in life. All is lost.

Similarly, this is the reason that difficulties come to a country. When what is needed by the people is lessened, when the fire of hunger burns in their stomachs, when the difficulties of hunger come, they forget the (good) qualities, and evil qualities develop in them.

A president or ruler, those who are in charge of looking after a country, must look at that engine and see if it has what it needs

---

2. *pasi vandāl, pattum parandu poitch* (T) When hunger comes, the ten will fly away. The ten may refer to the Ten Commandments.

for it to function. They must see if it needs water, oil, or air. They must check on the needs of the people of the country in an orderly way and keep them well supplied so they can have peace. Then there will be benefit, and no matter what comes, good will prevail; there will be goodness and prosperity. This is psychology, and this is what we should think about. If they (the people) are nurtured in this way, they will do what is good, but if they are not taken care of, they will explode and harm others. There will be no benefit, and others will be hurt.

Every person, every human being should think of this. This is the cause, the reason. The cause is this important point. This point will come. The most important point is that if man's needs are taken care of and if he is peaceful, then destruction and its evils will not come to that country. Man must think about other men. If he does duty to them with equality and peace, then that will be the kingdom of God—Justice.

Man must analyze himself; he must research into the two sections within him. He must analyze the two qualities within himself and understand the section of destruction and the section of progress. He must understand the two qualities and the two actions. Understanding these, he must discard the evil qualities and take the good qualities. He must act with those good qualities and make them grow.

If a king wants to dispense justice, he must be a king to his own house. He must be a king to his own life and to the country. He must rule his own heart. He must be the king to the world that is within him. If he wants to dispense justice, there must be only one Justice. Truth is Justice. That is Justice. That is God. That is Justice—God's throne. If one wants to dispense this Justice, he must understand the state that is within himself and then rule his own world with justice. He must be a king to his own world, and rule his own life. He can belong to any religion, any race, any scripture, or any kingdom, but if he has an attachment to a certain religion, he will not be able to dispense justice. There will be no justice. He will be unjust because he will have partiality towards his religion or towards some other attachment. He will be partial and favor his own side. He must consider both sides. "My religion" and "your religion" will be there. Both parties must be considered in the decision. If, because of his attachment, he gives a favorable decision to his side and is unjust to the other side, then his justice is finished, *poitch*.

Both sides will come, both sides will come to argue. In his kingdom two sides will come to explain (their position). He is the ruler of that world, the seat of justice. If his religion and another religion start fighting, saying "I, I," he is the one who must judge. Justice means that both sides must be given the proper justice. If he has an attachment to one side and favors it, then the other side will not have justice. If he favors his own side and makes a decision for the side of his attachment, there will be no justice for the other side. That is wrong. Then there is no justice.

When making a decision he must consider both sides—this is bad, that is good. For both, there is one Point—God. "There is only one Point for what you both have brought, and that one Point is Truth. For both of you there is only one Point. There is only One. That one Point is Justice." He (the king) will say, "What you have brought is a fault, and what you have brought is a lie." That one Justice is given so the fault can be removed, so that both will be right. There is one Point, one God, one Justice, one family, one prayer. That one (Point) is used for both sides. "Both of you have brought differences and separations. You! Cut away your differences. And you! Cut away your differences. Justice has no differences, God has no differences, Truth has no differences.

There is one God, one Power. That is a Power. There is no place for the form you bring. There is only God's form. That is a Power. There is no place for the separation of race that you bring. That (Power) has no separation. There is no room for the form, color, hue, or language that you bring. To that (Power), all languages are one point. It uses that one point of truth, that justice." You must show this, and say, "You, go and correct your fault. And you, go and correct your fault. There is only one point of justice." This is the way you become a king to yourself.

The next point...if you have an attachment to a woman or to wealth or to a possession or to a religion, a race, or status, then that attachment will affect the case. An opposite will come. One is good and one is bad, they are opposites. There are two forms, one is opposite and one is truth. There will always be an opposite that comes. One is attachment and the other is non-attachment. One is equality and one is selfishness. One is self-business love and the other is God's love, equal love. One is true love and one is selfish love, sex love, carnal love, music love. Pairs of opposites will come. In your life, there are two sections, and these two will always oppose one another.

When a case comes up, if you are attached to one side, you cannot be just. If you are attached to one side, you will be unfair to the other side. You must remain on the right side, and standing there, say to one, "This is wrong, and you must change this," and to the other say, "This is wrong, and you must change that," To both, you say, "This is this side, and that is that side. You must both understand and change." You must show, "This is the side of destruction; this is the side of goodness. Both of you must change." This must be controlled.

Fire brings a case on one side and Water brings a case on the other side. They are opposites. Both are opposites. Fire says, "Water wants to kill me." Water says, "Fire wants to destroy me." You must say, "Ah, *shari,* all right, what both of you did is wrong. You (Fire) can be beneficial, and you (Water) can be beneficial. Both of you can help man. Water, you stay in the pot. Fire, you stay under the pot. Both of you go. Both of you, do your duty. Do whatever duty is needed to help the people. Both of you can stay together in the same place. *Heat* and *cool.* Heat and cool can remain in the same place. You (Fire) can be there, and you (Water) can be there. Both of you can stay in one place. You are heat and you are cool. When cool is needed, you can give coolness. Do what is needed. Go! It is not necessary for you to be separate. Stay there in the correct way. The cool water can be there in the pot, and beneath that (is the fire), which can be used as needed by people. It is not necessary for you to fight." That is justice.

Like this, in one's own world there are so many problems that have to be solved. If one is a politician who has power and titles, and if he is attached to one religion, he will be unjust. That will create divisions. If he tries to dispense justice to all while being attached to one (section), whether it is an attachment to a wife, a child, a race, a religion, a color, or a language, he will not be able to do so. That will not be justice, it will be the opposite, injustice, and that will destroy the country. The country will be destroyed because of his unfair judgment due to his attachment. There will be suffering, there will be difficulties, and there will be poverty and destruction by fire. Justice will fail, and the fire of injustice will grow. Therefore, justice should not have an attachment to anything.

You can be anything. You can be an ignorant *gnāni,* a false *gnāni,* a science *gnāni,* or a true *gnāni.* But justice should not take sides with any one point. Whether it is your child or someone else's child, your wife or someone else's wife, your neighbor or your own born brother, there must be justice. Justice is Justice. That is Truth—God. That is Truth.

Your heart is your witness. Conscience[3] is the point. When your heart is the witness and when truth is justice, there will be no differences, and justice can be given. Whether you are a politician, a ruler, a beggar, or anything else, if you are in this state, where you act justly without attachment, if you keep justice as justice, then that is justice. If there is room for justice in your heart, you will prosper; you will not be destroyed. If a king of the country has that justice within him, he and the country will prosper. If a rich man has that justice within him, his wealth will be the wealth of grace—God's kingdom, the kingdom of justice, the kingdom of heaven. If a poor man has that wealth of justice in him, he will be God's son, and he will not be destroyed. He will have His wealth.

Only this is Justice, the Justice of God. He (God) has no form, shape, color, hue, race, religion, or differences. He has none of these. He is a Power, and that Power is Truth. That Truth is Justice. That Justice is the Light. That Light is God. That (God) rules and moves everything from within and without. It is a Power. That Power is within you, and when justice comes, you will understand this. When that wisdom, that justice, those qualities, and those actions come, you will understand this within yourself. It is not somewhere else, here or there, in the ocean, in the hills, in the mountains, or in the caves. Justice, truth, destruction, and progress are within you, within your own kingdom. Every human being should think of this.

Psychology is to know your self. That is psychology. Know the

---

3. conscience: In Tamil, the word for conscience is *manōchādchi,* a combination of *manam,* the heart, and *chādchi,* the witness. Thus, the conscience is the witness of the heart.

two qualities that are within you and know the two sections that are within you. One is unity, communaisam. One is the opposite of communaisam. The mind is opposite. You must understand the (two) qualities that are opposite to each other—the qualities of love, *naisam,* and the qualities of the system of communism. Understand the system and *naisam* which are opposites, and then give judgment. That will be very good. Then you will understand your life. You will understand what man is like, what a valuable person he is, how he is the leader for all lives, how he is the wise one for all creation, how he is the one who is just, the one with wisdom, the one who has equality, the one who gives peace to all lives, the one who gives tranquility to all lives, the one who treats all lives as his own life, and the one who comforts all lives.

Man. When these qualities come, he is man. The one who does this is God. The one who has these qualities is man. The one who does this is God. Therefore, it can be said that he is man-God. If he is man, then within man is God, and he is He. That is man-God. If he is a man, man's qualities are God's qualities, and that is God, man-God. That is man-God. When man reaches this state, when he has these qualities and this truth, that is God, man-God. We must think of this. When he knows this, and when this state and this justice come, he will have peace.

By analyzing ourselves, we will understand how to know Him. We will speak about this later. My love you.

❀[9]❀

Man's Form Changes According to His Qualities

March 13, 1982, Saturday 6:45 AM

If you act as an instrument of God, whatever comes will not affect you; He will bear it. Then you will be able to finish what you started. You must be the instrument, then He will be the One who is the Doer. That is the point.

Evil is everywhere, it is joined with you. When you set out to do something good, when you are the instrument to do a good duty, the opposite of it, evil, will oppose you. If the "I" sets out to do something, it will be difficult, but if you become an instrument (of God), the weight is His. Then it will be easy. You must think of this. This point is the point of psychology. This is the way you must realize wisdom and truth in your life.

My love you, my children. My love you, my children, my daughters, my sons, brothers, and sisters. Our life is God's psychology. He has placed two forms within His creations—wrong and right. He has created two forms, two bodies, two qualities, and two actions—good and bad. This is the point that works within man. There are two bodies. One body is good and one body is bad; one is the body of good qualities and one is the body of bad qualities. One action is a good action and one action is a bad action. Man can change these qualities. While

131

existing in this body itself, man must change this section.

When the bad qualities of deceit, scheming, treachery, jealousy, and envy come to him, he will change into a snake, the body of a snake. When he assumes the body of a snake he is poisonous, he is a snake. Truth is his enemy, his opponent. His work is to give the poison of evil. This is what this form does, those qualities do that. Even if goodness touches him, he will hiss, *shhhhhhs,* and strike back. This is what he will do.

What does a snake do? It kills others, it poisons them, that is the snake's body. If man changes into a snake, he will have the qualities of a snake, his form will be that of a snake, and he will enjoy doing its work.

Another quality he changes into is that of a tiger. What is the work of a tiger? When a tiger becomes hungry or when some adversity comes, it kills. It kills some other creation. That is its happiness. When man changes into a tiger, he has the qualities of a tiger. His form changes into that of a tiger, his qualities change into that of a tiger, and he enjoys murdering anything in the world. He will kill any creation and eat what he kills. That is the form he changes into. In that form he murders, and what he murders, he eats. He enjoys that. One is a tiger and the other is a tiger. He has the form of murder, and with that quality and in that house, he murders. This is psychology. He will do what is evil when he changes into those qualities. He will drink blood, he will murder, and he will eat flesh. He will eat the flesh of the world.

A lion has tremendous force and a leaping quality. It has anger, hastiness, and impatience. When man has those qualities, he changes into the form of a lion. When he changes into that form, he does that work. That is happiness to him. Murder is his pleasure. As soon as he acquires those evil qualities and changes his form, he will do that work, and that will give him pleasure. He will enjoy drinking blood. He will enjoy murder and killing.

Some animals, such as an elephant or a bear or some other dangerous animal, will not eat what they kill, but will still enjoy killing. They will strike and watch, just as a cat does. The cat catches a rat, watches it, lets it go a little, catches it again, torments it, and plays with it. Like that, if this cat-like quality comes (to a man), he will enjoy doing this. In this form, his qualities are that of a cat and his thoughts are that of a cat. When a cat catches a rat, it lets the rat go, watches it, catches it again, toys with it, and torments it. Some animals have these qualities. Like this, a man will hurt others, hurt their lives, watch them suffer, torment them, and cruelly strike again. Finally, he will finish them off, he will kill them. He will make men suffer, torment them, and finally kill them. This is his happiness. This is the happiness of the qualities of that form, that animal.

Some animals will watch you suffer. The elephant will crush you under its foot and then just watch you. Other animals have the quality of killing and eating what they kill.

Like this, there are four hundred trillion, ten thousand qualities that keep changing in man's body, in this *wrong body*. There are good qualities and bad qualities. There is a bad body and a good body. Within one body there are two bodies, one that has evil qualities and one that is God's body, the Light body. When (man's) qualities change into that Light body, he will do what is good, he will do what is good for all lives. He will comfort all lives and do duty to them. He will give peace to all lives. He will give justice to all lives on the path of truth, the straight path. He will give tranquility, compassion, love, and equality. He has the two qualities—wrong and right. When he has the right qualities, he does that (what is right), but when he has the bad qualities, every quality becomes a demon, a ghost, or a vampire that drinks blood. He drinks the blood of other lives. He tortures other lives, kills women, rapes beautiful women; he does this and he does that. These are the vampire qualities. All the qualities of magic, mesmerism, the power, the shakti of the "I," and the energy of the cells change him.

When he is like this, when these evil qualities are working within him, he has one of the ninety-six crazinesses. He is crazy. Every thought becomes a craziness. He has differences, insanity, anger, deceit, treachery, obstinacy, jealousy, and envy. These become the animal qualities, where one is jealous of another and one kills another. One who has this bad quality will enjoy killing and eating others, just like animals kill and eat each other. These are his actions. Making others suffer is natural for him; this makes him happy. There are, like this, these bad qualities and this bad body.

There are the two qualities of good and bad, and there are the two bodies. Man does the work of both sections. In the bad section, he changes into four hundred trillion, ten thousand different qualities. Every thought takes a form. He changes into the form of whatever thought he has and, in that form, goes on the bad path. This is his happiness. A man who is in this state can be called crazy. He does this because of the connection between his mind, emotions, nature, and thoughts. His thoughts evoke a certain quality in him. He changes into its actions and form, and he does the work of each animal. He takes on the countless qualities of monkeys, donkeys, goats, bulls, dogs, foxes, snakes, scorpions, four-legged animals, elephants, birds, eagles, and vultures. Some have these qualities.

There are some animals that are afraid, that have the qualities of fear. Certain animals may have the thought of killing, but when they go to kill, they become afraid. If a forceful animal such as a lion appears, they become frightened. If a fox, who kills by means of trickery, encounters a forceful animal like a lion, it becomes afraid, and that fear makes it run and hide.

Similarly, if a man who has this quality, this evil state of wanting to kill, sees a more forceful opponent, he becomes frightened. As soon as he sees him, fear comes, and he runs and hides. Some people shiver, some hide; they have those animal qualities. In their thoughts, those four-legged and two-legged beings fear that demons and ghosts are coming to kill them. As soon as that fear comes, as soon as that quality comes, as soon as a forceful opponent comes, they run and hide. Some hide under the bed, some crouch here and there, and some hide where no one can see them. That section comes to those who have this quality. When they have those evil qualities, that fear comes.

Some forceful animals, such as the lion or rhinoceros, will murder straight-on. Some dangerous animals will fight head-on. If those qualities come in a man, he will behave like those animals, and will enjoy it.

Like this, each quality changes him, and he does that work. As soon as he changes into that form, as soon as he changes into the qualities of that evil form, he will do that work. When you observe this, you will see that murder, killing others, and making others sad give him pleasure. That action, that evil quality makes him happy. That is what he enjoys.

Like this, there are two that work in the one body. One is the good thoughts and good qualities. The other is bad, the bad qualities. When good thoughts come (within man), he will change into God's qualities, the quality of compassion, the quality of love, the quality of equanimity, and God's three thousand gracious qualities. He will have justice, conscience, and truthful ways. He will consider the lives of others as his own life, the prosperity of others as his own prosperity, the hunger of others as his own hunger, the suffering of others as his own suffering, the house of others as his own house, the property of others as his own property, the state of others as his own state, the body of others as his own body, the blood of others as his own blood, and the flesh of others as his own flesh. When that good section and these good qualities work in him, every good quality will do what is good. He will do the work that God does. He will change into God's form. He will change into the form of His three thousand gracious qualities. Step by step, he will change into these and do all his work with God's ninety-nine *wilāyats,* His power, actions, conduct, and behavior. He does his beneficial work with those good qualities.

Bad qualities take the forms of the four hundred trillion, ten thousand spiritual animal powers, *tattwas.* In those forms man will do the prayer, *vanakkam,* of animals, the prayer of demons, the prayer of ghosts, the prayer of maya, the prayer of satan, the prayer of birds, the prayer of jinns, the prayer of the elements, the prayer of earth, the prayer of fire, the prayer of water, and the prayer of air. His thoughts keep changing. Every attachment is connected to his flesh. There is a connection in his body to the earth, water, air, and ether, the sun and the moon, and because of this connection, his qualities change. As a result, he will do that work, the evil work. There are two qualities in man, there are two bodies, and one face reveals both. In one body, there are two sections. Man acts in these ways because of these two sections.

In this state God's Power and truth must come, or a wise man, an Insān Kāmil, must come and show him the connection to the two sections within. He must cut away the connection to the bad section. He must guide him and show him with wisdom: This is wrong, this is right. He will show: This is murder, this is goodness, that is evil, this is a good point, that is a bad point. He will cut each quality, he will cut each evil. He will explain and cut, and change that into the *good body, God's body*. He will change his (man's) qualities into the form that does good duty. He will change him into the section where he considers all lives as his own life, and will dispel the qualities of the sections of murder and evil.

There is one Point, man-God. He will change into those actions. Man will acquire the qualities, actions, and justice of God. Instead of changing into the form of satan, man becomes one form, God's form, the Light form. Instead of changing into the four hundred trillion, ten thousand forms, there is one form, the Light form, the Truth form, God's form. That form is Light, and that Light has resplendent wisdom, resplendent qualities, resplendent purity, and resplendent perfection.

It is rare to find an Insān Kāmil in this world, but if you can find such a one, then it will be easy to change this form and its (evil) qualities. If you obediently follow him, what was difficult will become easy. It will become easier and easier and easier. One by one, one by one, one by one, you can change each thing. This is psychology.

In this (present) state, every quality and every form gives man pleasure. Murder is his happiness, killing is happiness, causing suffering to others is happiness, making someone miserable is happiness, taking someone's house is happiness, chasing someone into the jungle is happiness, murdering someone's wife and children is happiness. To do the work of many, many ghosts, devils, evil beings, animals, birds, reptiles, and snakes gives him pleasure. It makes him happy to do this. Like that, he does the work of the particular quality. As soon as that state comes, as soon as that animal quality comes, he does that work. When the qualities of a ghost come, he does that work. When the qualities of a blood-

sucking demon, *asura,* come, he does that. When the qualities of
a man who eats other men come, he does that. When he takes on
the quality of an animal that catches other animals, he catches
others. This is what he does.

There are these two qualities and two forms in a man. Good
and evil have existed in him from the beginning. Evil qualities (do
evil). Good qualities develop goodness—they will never do what
is evil. This is psychology, God's wisdom psychology. These two
sections develop from the time you are born. You need to understand these. They grow from your actions, your qualities, your
sight, your associations, and your thoughts. If you join with good
people, wise people, good friends, and good men, and make their
qualities and actions yours, then you can change to their ways.
Then you can change to that section.

In the same way, to grow a flowering plant, a fruit tree, or a
vegetable, we must plant it in the earth. To grow a tree, we mix
fertilizer and chemicals together and add them to the earth. This
is the soil it grows in. Like this, this body also grows in the dirt
of earth, fire, water, and air. To grow a flower, a flowering plant,
a fruit tree, or a vegetable, many different kinds of dirt are com-
bined to make fertilizer. Once we put this (fertilizer) on the earth,
the earth eats the fertilizer and gives its essence to the plant or
tree. As soon as it is given, the tree accepts it. When this is given,
what happens? The essence joins with the tree, those qualities join
with it, the dirt joins with it. Later, the fruit reveals the taste. That
fruit has changed. The tree grows in the dirt, it takes its nourishment from the soil, the water, fire, air, and earth, but when the
fruit comes, that has changed. The taste has come.

Like this, a flowering plant is also planted in dirt and given
fertilizer. When the flower blooms, when that beauty comes, the
fragrance is revealed, and the dirt is no longer present. The plant

was given fertilizer and grew in the dirt, but the fragrance has no dirt. There is no dirt in the fragrance of the flower, and there is no dirt in the fruit which has changed into the taste.

Similarly, this body is made up of earth, fire, water, and air. The thoughts are the fertilizer we put on this body. The body grows from these. The heart is also made up of earth, fire, water, blood, and air, and grows from these. However its essence must change. The flower of this *qalb,* inner heart, must change in the same way the flower changed into the fragrance. Although it grows in the dirt of the body, which is full of chemicals and the elements, the heart, the flower of the heart, must change. When it changes, opens, and becomes beautiful, it no longer has the connection to the body. It has been transformed into the fragrance— the fragrance of God, the fragrance of Truth. If that fragrance develops, it will give peace to everyone. It will give peace and the fragrance of love to everyone. Everyone will be enchanted by its fragrance. The heart must change into that flower.

The body grows from many chemicals, from dirt, fertilizer, and earth. It grows from fertilizer, dirt, earth, fire, water, and air. A tree also grows like this. A man's life must change just as a tree changes. His thoughts, his life, and his body must change. When the taste develops in a fruit, when the fruit changes into the taste, there is no dirt. Although man's life and his birth are formed from dirt—his soul, his wisdom, his qualities, that truth and justice do not have that dirt. He must change to that section.

The body is composed of maya, fire, arrogance, karma, *tāra-han, singhan,* and *sūran,* earth, woman, and gold, desire, anger, miserliness, attachment, and fanaticism, intoxicants, lust, theft, murder, and falsehood, the five elements, the thoughts, and the forces of illusion. These are all mixed together in the body when it is formed. The body eats these and grows. It feeds and grows on their essence, and then they are destroyed.

Similarly, truth must destroy these (bad) qualities. The earth must be destroyed and changed into taste and fragrance, just as a flower changes and becomes fragrant. Like this, these shaktis must be destroyed so that wisdom can grow, and the *qalb* can blossom and give fragrance. Before its state changes, everything is mixed in this body. This must be changed. If it is not changed, it will do evil and will not be beneficial for anything. Only if it changes will it do what is good. You must think of this.

This is how an Insān Kāmil, a Shaikh, will change you. He will change these qualities that grow in dirt, this body that grows in dirt, and bring you to the state of justice, truth, and wisdom. The work of the Insān Kāmil is to bring you to this state. That is the Father's section, to change that to God.

This is true psychology, God's psychology. This is what we must understand. You must understand every point.

A'ūdhu billāhi minash-shaitānir-rajīm.
I seek refuge in God from the accursed satan.

Bismillāhir-Rahmānir-Rahīm.
In the name of God, the Most Compassionate, the Most Merciful.

Transcend the Animal Horoscopes and Discover the True Horoscope of Man

March 14, 1982, Sunday 9:00 AM

We have been talking about the two qualities: one is the quality that does good, and the other is the quality that does evil. These two sections are in the one body.

Good actions belong to heaven, to goodness, to the kingdom of God. That is heaven, peace. It is the peace and tranquility of life. That place is the kingdom of God, heaven.

Evil qualities cause sorrow and suffering to the emotions of the mind, showing both happiness and sadness. It shows both of these. That is hell.

In life, one shows heaven, it shows goodness. The other is the *hellboard*,[1] it shows hell. These two qualities of good and evil live together in the body. Man must learn about these two sections that are within him. He must realize, learn, and understand them. Understanding this is psychology. The wisdom to understand this must develop in man. That wisdom, the wisdom of the soul, must develop in him. God's qualities must be reflected in him; that wisdom, that quality, that action, that behavior, that goodness, that love, compassion, and patience must develop in him.

---

1. hellboard: Bawa Muhaiyaddeen ☻ often referred to the attractions of the world as advertisements or billboards for hell.

When God's duty and His qualities dawn in man, when wisdom appears, all his actions will be the good actions of the kingdom of heaven. He will have equanimity, peace, equality, and tranquility in his life. The life he leads in this world and the benefits he has earned for the next world are the kingdom that he will have within him. He will understand this within himself. These qualities are God's qualities.

The other quality he acts with is in accordance with the ways of the world, and is caused by thoughts that arise from the emotions of the mind. These are the qualities that display the actions of hell, the actions of the shaktis, the energies of the elements, the demons, and torpor. When these energies and qualities develop, the qualities of the animals, the birds, the reptiles, the snakes, the fish, the four-legged animals, the viruses, the cells, the blood-sucking vampires, and the other created beings will develop in him. These shaktis destroy one another. One shakti controls another shakti. One shakti kills another shakti. One cell kills another cell. One torpor attacks and kills another torpor. One virus controls and kills another virus. One quality controls and kills another quality. One action is controlled by another action with the pride of "I, I." In this way, every thought, every shakti develops a (corresponding) quality within him, and one attacks the other.

One bird kills another bird. Another bird eats a different kind of bird. Fire burns a tree or something else. That is its work. Water floods. It uproots trees, or washes away a mound of dirt or anything else that stands in its way. Air breaks down whatever is in its way. An earthquake turns the land into sea or the sea into land. This is the way that every shakti of earth, fire, water, air, ether, mind, and desire takes part in the section of destruction.

When he (man) changes into the state of a particular shakti, energy, he becomes that shakti. When he changes into the shakti of fire, he becomes fire and does the work of fire. That quality comes. Sometimes he does the work of water, and destroys and shatters whatever is in his way. Sometimes he does the work of forceful air. Sometimes he does the work of the earth; he has patience, peace, and equanimity. Sometimes he does the work of the "I" and the "you," saying, "I, I." Sometimes he does the work of ether, illusion, or mesmerism.

Sometimes he does the work of the elements, sometimes he does the work of the qualities of demons, fascination, hypnotism, and magic. He changes his form according to the particular quality. Just as a chameleon changes its color from green to red to white, his actions change and change according to the quality that is in his mind. He takes different forms. Whatever quality comes, he acts in that way.

When the quality of a fish comes, he acts like a fish. He jumps and swims in the water, saying, "I am strong. I am clever." He does the work of a fish, and with that quality, with that shakti, and using the ego of the "I," he tries to get a title.

Some people fly in the air like a bird. They say, "I am clever," and try to get a title for it. They have this quality and do this work of the air.

Some do the work of an elephant. When the arrogant quality of the elephant comes, they display the strength of the elephant. They act with this animal quality and attempt to gain a title for it, claiming, "I! None is stronger than I."

Some like to box like a monkey. They jump and leap here and there, up and down, and they fight. In this monkey section, with that monkey quality, they try to get a title, claiming, "I am a clever person."

Some have the quality of a tiger. They jump, catch, and run like a tiger. They take on that section and behave like a tiger or a lion.

They take on the section of each animal. With the quality of a poisonous snake, they bite, kill, and frighten others with the claim, "I am the greatest." They act like a pig, a rhinoceros, a dog, a fox, a cat, a rat, an eagle, or a vulture. They fly like a vulture, searching for corpses to eat. They fly in the sky like an eagle, seeking things on the earth, such as a snake, that they can catch as their prey.

Like this, he (man) performs the actions of the countless birds, animals, fish, and viruses. He changes into these sections of devils, ghosts, and demons, takes on their shaktis, and runs, dances, and sings like them. He acts like this and gains titles for it. He does this with these qualities. This is how some commit murder and how some become arsonists who burn down the city. They change into that quality, and do that work.

It is in this state that man acquires titles, praise, and fame. They call these miracles. They say, "This is worship, this is prayer," and begin to worship these actions. They take on the qualities of bulls, goats, donkeys, and horses, and they do what they do. They eat and plow the world like a bull, they jump like a goat or cow, they jump like a kangaroo on two legs.

Like that, man takes on the qualities of these animals and other created beings, gains titles for it, and displays his strength in this world, in this section. The energy of each thought changes him. That energy changes him. He takes on its section and acts according to it, he acts according to that thought. That thought controls him, that quality controls him, every section controls him. His mind controls him and changes him from a man into an animal, from doing the actions of a man to doing the actions of an animal, a demon, a ghost, fire, or air. Because of this, his life is hell, and he does everything with evil qualities. His form changes into whatever his thoughts are at a particular time, and he does that work. This is hell.

There are two forms. One is the form of a man who acts like an animal. The other is the form of a man who lives as a man, with man's qualities, and does what is good. In the form of a man who acts like an animal, he does what is evil. These two qualities that do two kinds of work are within his one form. When he does what is evil, he changes into thousands of forms; he changes forms over and over again, like a chameleon. When he has good qualities there is one God, one Point. God is one Point. He will do the one work of the qualities of His kingdom. In the other section, man will take many different forms. However, for a human being, an Insān Kāmil, there is plenitude, perfection, light, and God.

Man has these two forms. One is hell, one is heaven. One is good. One is bad. One is a life of plenitude. One is temporary—his life is one of ignorance, and he is in the depths of hell. Both of these dwell within the same man. He must keep checking both of these qualities, "This is the quality that commits sins, and this is the good action and good quality that does good." The understanding of both of these qualities is psychology. He should learn to understand them both. Every man has these two qualities within him.

Man has six different wisdoms within him. *Pahut arivu,* divine analytic wisdom, is within him. Even though he is a man and has one head, every quality has the body of earth, the body of fire, the body of air, the body of water, and the body of illusion.

He also has the body of man:

> The body of man is light.
> The head of man is God.
> The life of man is truth.

The wisdom of man is the good qualities of God.

This light form is the sign, *adayālam*, of man.
This form has one head. This life, this body has one head.

There is another body that is inside him. That other body has
five heads; every thought has the heads of earth, fire, water, air,
and ether. These are five heads. A man has six heads inside. Outside he has one head, but inside he has the six heads of the six
lives: earth life, fire life, water life, air life, ether or maya life, the
glitters, and human life, which is the light life, the soul—God's
Light—it is the pure soul, the *rūh*, the light-soul.

The qualities of the soul behave in one way. The other five
behave in a different way. The five are joined with the world, and
this (soul) is joined with God.

This soul is connected to God, and the five are connected to
the world. Within the earth exist water, air, fire, and maya, which
is the ether—torpor. All the shaktis of torpor are there, they are
shaktis. But this (God) is a Power, this is a Power that is within
man. The others are all energies, shaktis, cells, but this is a Power.
These shaktis are made into four hundred trillion, ten thousand
spiritual gods. Every thought takes form and becomes a god.
What is inside becomes a god outside. The inside quality becomes
a form on the outside. The inside action becomes an action on the
outside. Their form can be seen. It is like a mirror. Man's thought
becomes his god. This is the god he creates. If he has fanaticism
inside, he becomes an elephant outside. If he is pulling the world
inside, he becomes a bull outside. If he is a monkey inside, he is a
monkey outside. If he is a snake inside, he is a snake outside. If he
is a rat inside, he is a rat outside.

This state becomes a form. The inner form becomes the outer

form, and that form becomes his spiritual prayer. He prays to his own qualities, his own evil qualities. When man has beautiful qualities, that is God, that is a Power: beautiful qualities, beautiful actions, beautiful truth, the beautiful soul, the one Point. That is God, that is a Power. Man believes in that Power. But when he has all the other qualities within him, he prays to those.

This is psychology. We should understand this psychology. The wisdom to study and understand both of these is within man. We must think of this.

Within every human being there are these six lives, their qualities and actions. One is *insān,* man, and one is *hayawān,* animal. There is *insān-hayawān,* man-animal, and there is man-God. If man has His qualities, that is God. If his qualities are Light, that is His Power. If he has the qualities of God, he is complete. He is within God and God is within him. His history is within God and God's history is within him. That point is like this. We need to think of this. Thinking about this and learning this within ourselves is psychology. We need to understand this.

My love you, my children, grandchildren, granddaughters, grandsons, brothers, sisters. It is not easy to learn and understand this. All the learning of the world is mixed within this study of psychology: the sixty-four sexual arts, the sixty-four arts and sciences, the ninety-six *tattwas,* potentialities, the eighteen puranas, the six shastras,[2] the thirty-six *tattwas* of the demons and jinns, the ninety-six *tattwas* of man, the twenty-five thousand nerves, the four thousand, four hundred and forty-eight diseases, and the two hundred and forty-eight pieces of bone.

Like this, we have to understand these in our eyes, ears, nose, body, marrow, nerves, blood, air, in the fire, in the flesh, in the

---

2. shastras (T) Six philosophical systems in Hinduism; horoscopes.

hair follicles, in our visions, in our thoughts, in our tongue, in our speech, in our sounds, in our nose, and in our smell. We have to understand each section, in the feces, in the urine, and in the food. We have to understand the benefit each gives. We need to know what is wrong and right in each food, what is wrong and right in each glance, what is wrong and right in each sound, what is wrong and right in each smell, what is wrong and right in each taste, and what is wrong and right in each speech. We must see what is good and what is bad in our giving and receiving. We must see what is good and bad in our behavior and what is good and bad in our conduct. We must understand what our actions and qualities are. There is good and bad in our thoughts, there is good and bad in our actions, in our sight, and in our intentions. In our qualities, there are good qualities and bad qualities. We need to understand all of these. There is wrong and right in race, religion, scripture, philosophy, dogma, color, and languages. We must understand equality, selfishness, differences, self-business, wisdom, and ignorance.

When you understand these and become peaceful, when you find tranquility, when you make a connection between good qualities, a good state, God, and yourself, then that is a good quality. When you connect with the truth, when you live with the fullness of truth, and when you achieve plenitude in life, you will know God who is Life within life. When you merge with Him: life merges with God's life, actions merge with His actions, truth merges with His truth, conduct merges with His conduct, sight merges with His sight, speech merges with His speech, and the body merges with His body. When all the qualities and actions are merged with His, then you are good, you are a man, a human being, an Insān Kāmil. Then you will act with those (good) actions.

You will act according to whatever you are merged with. Evil qualities will do what is evil. An evil vision will see evil and be happy. An evil mind will do the evil work of the mind. Like this, if you change and your actions become evil, that will be your sorrow. There will be both joy and sorrow. You will call sorrow a joy and joy a sorrow. You need to think of this.

My love you. This is psychology. For each one to learn about himself within himself is psychology. If you have a Gnāna Shaikh, an Insān Kāmil, he may be able to give you certain explanations. It is easy to become a guru, it is easy to become a shaikh, it is easy to read books, and it is easy to read the puranas.

When a wind blows in an open space, it makes a howling sound, *ooh-ahoooo*. If you blow air through a pipe that has holes in certain places, it will produce different sounds. If you have a large pipe and blow air through it, there is the sound, *ooooh*. When you have a smaller pipe there will be a lesser sound, *oooh*. If you have an even smaller one, it will have less force, *ooh*. Another pipe will make the sound of *shhhhh*. Each pipe will make many different musical sounds. If there are some leaves in the pipe as the air goes through it, it will make the sound, *nngnnggg*. If there is something else in the pipe, it will make a different sound. As you blow the air into a smaller and smaller space, it will have a higher pitch. When air is in an open space, it makes a howling sound. But as you bring the air through smaller and smaller and smaller points, the sound will be different. Air can make many different kinds of musical sounds. This is the way it might be.

Like this, when your qualities run like the wind in the open space, they will howl. You must *check* them. If you keep *checking* them, *checking* them, *checking* them, and bring them to the right place within yourself, you can produce many different sounds. If you can bring them to the Point of God, then you can understand the Resonance and Resplendence of that All-Pervasive Treasure, the Omnipresent Being, the Solitary One, *illAllāhu*, the One who is alone. You can understand His truth within yourself. If you can shrink the forces within yourself and make them small, if you can open your wisdom, shrink yourself, make yourself into a tiny point, into one point, an atomic point, if you can come to God's Point, then within that you will understand His sound, His three thousand gracious qualities, His ninety-nine *wilāyats*, attributes, and His countless speeches and actions that are within you. Within yourself you will understand your soul and God's *Tattwa*, His Power.

When you stand in the open space of illusion and listen to that music, your understanding will be in accordance with the qualities you possess and what you have learned. You must shrink these, reduce them, and take the one Point. Otherwise, you will hear the sounds of "my religion, your religion, my race, your race, my scripture, your scripture, my color, your color, my language, your language." You will have those within you. You will have the language of the *tattwas*, potentialities, of the animals; you will have the qualities of the animals and the *tattwas* of the animals, the qualities of the birds and the *tattwas* of the birds. If you have these actions, you are not a human being, you have changed into another form.

You need to change this form and make it small. You have changed into an animal, and you are looking at the animal horoscopes, shastras. Only animals have these horoscopes. When you look at these horoscopes, the animals are there. You change into an animal, and then try to read your astrological chart, but you cannot see your (real) horoscope. You need to discover what the horoscope of man is. Man's horoscope is psychology. You have to correctly look into this horoscope.

My love you. You are a *microbe,* you are the twenty-seven stars, *nadchattiram.* The twenty-seven stars are inside you. There are twenty-seven stars and twenty-seven letters, *hurūf,* within you. Your body is made up of the twenty-seven letters, starting with *alif.* The twenty-seven letters are those twenty-seven stars. There are the twelve zodiac signs, *rasis.* You are the book of astrology, you are the horoscope. The two nostrils, two ears, two eyes, the mouth, the two openings below, the navel, and the *'arsh,*[3] throne of God, and *kursī,*[4] eye of wisdom, are the twelve openings. Two must be opened. Of the other ten openings, one, the navel, has been cut and sealed. You are functioning with nine openings—two eyes, two nostrils, two ears, one mouth, and the two openings below. These are the nine planets, *nava kirahangal,* that are controlling you. There are twelve zodiac signs. The animal qualities, maya, and glitters that are in the nine planets are pulling and controlling you.

These are the planets that influence you—the eyes, ears, nose, mouth, and the two below. If you can conquer these, they will no longer have any control over you, you will control them. If you can control the eyes, if you can control the ears, if you can control the nose, if you can control the mouth, and if you can control the two openings below, then you will not be controlled by them. If you are not controlled by these planets, the other two openings will be opened. The *'arsh* and the *kursī* will be opened to you. When they are opened, you are the kingdom of God. You are God. You are the kingdom of God, and you can see everything.

When you control these planets, the five elements, the *pan-*

---

3. *'arsh* (A) The throne of God located on the crown of the head; the plenitude from which God rules.

4. *kursī* (A) The eye of wisdom located on the center of the forehead, where Allāh's *Nūr,* Light, was impressed on Adam ☉.

jāngam, will be controlled. *Alif, lām, mīm, hā',* and *dāl*[5] are the five letters. Earth, fire, water, air, and ether. *Al-hamd.* The five letters are the *panjāngam,* astrological almanac. Earth, fire, water, air, and ether. In Tamil, they say Shakti and Sivan. Adam ⊕ and Hawwā' ⊕ (creation, earth). Fire is known as Akkinibagavan. Air is known as Vāyubagavān. Water is known as Varunabagavān, and ether is Āhāyavani, or Maya Shakti. These are controlling you. These are the *panjāngam.* Maya, illusion, is the *panjangam.* This is the *panjādcharam,* the five letters, the heart, the one fistful of earth, *oru pidi man.* These five letters make up the astrology and horoscopes which control and disturb you and make you suffer. The heart is made up of these five letters.

You need to look at the sixth letter, the Light. It will not make you suffer. We need to think of this. You are the *panjāngam,* you are the horoscope, you are man, you are the animal, you are the demon, and you are God. You are the wise man and you are the ignorant man. Hell is within you, heaven is within you, joy is within you, sorrow is within you, God is within you, God's kingdom is within you, the kingdom of hell is within you. You must know all this. You have to learn all this within yourself, and understand it.

Understanding this is psychology. Understanding yourself is God's psychology. Asking questions such as, "Did you sleep? Did you wake up? Did you go with a woman? Did you go here? Did you go there? Did you eat?" is not psychology, not true psychology. "Did you wake up? What did your husband do? What did the children do? Did you eat? Did you wake up? How did you sleep? How did you sit? How did you cry? What did you see? Show how

---

5. *alif, lām, mīm, hā',* and *dāl* (A) Five letters of the Arabic alphabet which make up the innermost heart of man and, when transformed, become the praise of Allāh.

you did all these things," is not psychology. Everyone has the learning of psychology within himself. This is wisdom. We must try to learn what qualities are within us. This is truth, this is the way to find peace. When one understands all of this within himself, he will realize peace and tranquility.

My love you, my children, grandchildren, granddaughters, brothers, sisters. With wisdom we must change into these (good) qualities. We must search for wisdom and change into these qualities so we can have peace and equality and gain victory in our life. This is what you must think about. If you change to the section of God, then we can talk about that connection. If you change into these qualities, actions, and conduct, then we can talk about the connection that the daughter and son will have with the Father. We can talk about what kind of Being He is.

Have you seen a rose flower? All kinds of fertilizer, as well as dirt and eggshells are put on the plant. We put all this foul-smelling fertilizer, dirt, and eggshells on the plant. It gives it calcium. Have you seen what the flower does? The flower does not change into this dirt. It has a beautiful fragrance at all times. It retains its fragrance until it dies, is that not so? It does not change into the stench of the manure. From the time it blooms until the time it dies, it remains fragrant. Understand? It lives in the midst of stench, but does not have the stench. Understand?

Even though the flower grows from and lives in the dirt, its actions are not altered. It lives this way until it dies. A flower can do that. It is rooted in the dirt, yet its fragrance and beauty remain unchanged in the midst of that stench. Like that, if you, with certitude and determination, come to that (unchanging) state, you can remain like that forever. No matter how much the dirt of the world surrounds you, you do not have to change to its state. All of that is below. The fragrance is above. The beauty and fragrance are above. Everything else is below, beneath your feet. The world and its actions are beneath your feet. The truth and the fragrance are above. You should think of this.

If you remain unchanged, then whatever is below will not affect you. The world will not affect you, it is below. The fragrance and beauty are above, and the world is beneath your feet. The truth is in your heart, beauty is in your heart, and the Light—that fragrance—is in your face, in your sight, and in your qualities.

Thank you.

A'ūdhu billāhi minash-shaitānir-rajīm.
I seek refuge in God from the accursed satan.

Bismillāhir-Rahmānir-Rahīm.
In the name of God, the Most Compassionate, the Most Merciful.

The Disease Lives Within You: Cut It Away with Wisdom

March 15, 1982, Monday 6:55 AM

M. R. Bawa Muhaiyaddeen ☺ addresses an auto mechanic.

M. R. Bawa Muhaiyaddeen ☺: The mechanic is not yet ready to do the repairs. The *mechanic work,* this *body mechanic work,* is not completed. We have not learned enough. How can either of us do these two (kinds of mechanic work), how can we talk about these two kinds of repairs? How can we speak about it? I do not know how to take this (body) apart, see which parts are satisfactory, and then reassemble it correctly. A mechanic should know this well. I do not know about the mind parts, the heart parts, the nerves, the energies, the cells, and the *nuts.* How can we talk about this? You have not finished learning and I have not finished learning, so how can we say we are great mechanics?

Mechanic: If he doesn't know, nobody knows!

M. R. Bawa Muhaiyaddeen ☺: Who is there in this world that knows everything and has learned everything? It is difficult to find such a one. There are those who know about their one-span stomach. They know only about their stomach, but do not fully know about even one of the nine openings. They do not know which parts are *dangerous,* which parts need to be replaced, which parts are all right, and which parts are defective. They do not know which valve has gone bad in the urinary tract, which

155

valve works correctly, and which valve is worn out. In the colon where there is fecal arrogance, they do not know which valve is all right or whether the valve is open or closed. One time it (the feces) comes, one time it is stopped, constipated. One time they may need to take medicine, one time they may need to drink water, and one time they may need to take pills. They do not know which valve is worn out.

One time a tooth may be loose, another time a tooth may have a cavity. They do not know how to maintain those parts. The tongue praises, ridicules, grumbles, criticizes, extols, tastes, and speaks good and bad. They have not found out which parts have gone bad. The nose smells fragrances or bad odors, it smells this or that, or it does not smell anything at all. They do not know what part is in danger of losing its ability to smell. They do not know which is good, which is bad, or which valve, part, or nut is defective.

Sometimes the ear hears, sometimes it does not hear, sometimes the sound is good, sometimes the sound is bad, sometimes the sound is heard as *ehhhhh*. The eyes are like this, the nose is like this, the ears are like this. They do not know which part or which nerve is worn or which nut is loose.

Which parts of the mind are worn? Are the valves deteriorating, is the mind failing, is the heart weakening, are the nerves deteriorating, is the air less, or is the fire less? What parts are weak, what section is diminished, what section is increased? We have not yet discovered this, so how can we call ourselves mechanics? How can we speak to the world about that?

When we eat something sour, it sears the tongue; the acid eats into our tongue. Like this, when we talk about God, when we talk about life, when we talk about peace, when we talk about tranquility, when we talk about truth, or when we talk about evil, this talk will be the same as eating something sour—the acid will sear our tongue. Our *love* will cause us suffering. When we speak like this we cause suffering to ourselves. It is speech that is without understanding. It is speech that causes suffering to our own life and to our own soul.

My love you, my *tambi*, younger brother, mechanic *tambi*. My love you, Guru Bawa Muhaiyaddeen who is speaking wisdom, *gnānam*, who is talking about God. You should both learn well that speaking without understanding has no benefit, that it is like the tongue when we eat something sour. The two mechanics should do the mechanic work in the proper way. One is the *motor mechanic* and the other is the *body motor,* the *heart motor mechanic.* Both should do the repairs properly. If this is done, then we can speak about it.

One (motor) is a life motor, the other is a gas motor. A (gas) motor needs fire, oil, gas, and water. The motor of the body needs earth, fire, iron, and air; these must be put into that machine so it can work properly. It needs fire, earth, a body, gas, oil, air, and water. This is the way that motor is. Each section flies around in the monkey mind. Life also flies around and around. We need to hold onto the steering wheel to drive this (life motor), and we need to hold onto the steering wheel to drive that (car motor). Are the steering wheel, the brakes, and the axle okay? Are we looking where we are going? We have to drive our life in this way. We have to learn this properly so we can go on our journey, the journey of our soul. One is the path of the journey of the soul and the other is the road (for the journey of the car). Accidents can happen on both of these roads. If, at any time, we are inattentive or careless or not looking, accidents can happen on either of these (paths). We have to watch, be careful, and understand.

Both have things that get old, parts that wear out. The valves get worn and cause danger. We have to learn well about these. This is psychology. This mechanic work is psychology. We must correctly learn about the two sections. One is the motor of the section of the world, and one is the motor of the section of the soul. We should understand both of these well. We must learn from a good mechanic the correct way to do the mechanic work. We must learn how to complete our journey in the proper way. You must learn how to go on your journey in the correct way so you can get to the right place. This is important. Each person must learn the correct way to travel and reach his destination. That will be good.

If one has not learned to get there by himself, what is the use of his gathering people and taking them along with him? If he takes everyone with him, accidents will happen. That is guru business, the mechanic business of one who has not learned, of one who has not corrected himself.

We must learn this mechanic work well. *Tambi,* do you understand? Bawa Muhaiyaddeen, do you understand? We must try to understand and do what is right for our life. If you do not understand this, it is craziness. If we do not understand this, we are crazy. Bawa Muhaiyaddeen, if you do not understand this, you are crazy. Do you understand?

There are many kinds of crazinesses: love craziness, lust craziness, sex craziness, arts craziness, science craziness, wisdom craziness, ignorance craziness, house craziness, woman craziness, earth craziness, gold craziness, wealth craziness, children craziness, race craziness, scripture craziness, religion craziness, language craziness, spiritual craziness, hunger craziness, illness craziness, disease craziness, status craziness, fame craziness, people craziness, blood ties craziness, relatives craziness, attachments craziness, title craziness, occult powers craziness, miracles craziness, the craziness for property and possessions.

There is political craziness, guru craziness, poetry craziness, writing craziness, author craziness, learning craziness, position craziness, and music craziness. All of these are crazinesses. There is travel craziness, rounding craziness, mountain climbing craziness, sea travel craziness, craziness for ships, the craziness to run, the craziness to box, the craziness to hit, and the craziness to murder.

Like this, there are countless crazinesses. This craziness is the world. This world is crazy. Every man has this craziness within him, every creation has one of these sections of craziness: beauty craziness, joy craziness, sorrow craziness, suffering craziness, happiness craziness, liquor craziness, drugs craziness, marijuana craziness, drinking craziness. There is the craziness of sorrow, sadness, and troublesome thoughts. Every thought that appears has a craziness. There is husband craziness, children craziness, and wife craziness. Like this, there are countless crazinesses. These crazinesses are within you and are causing you to suffer. Without understanding, you cannot do this mechanic work correctly.

There is one-quarter craziness, one-half craziness, three-quarters craziness, and full craziness. There are some who are caught by one-quarter craziness, some who are caught by one-half craziness, and some who are caught by three-quarters craziness. These crazinesses make one suffer. If full craziness comes, there is nothing for him. There is no sorrow for him. Everything is finished, he will throw everything away. Because of that (full) craziness, he will not be aware of anything, it is finished. That is full craziness.

In life, wisdom and *gnānam* are also like this. Everything has either one-quarter craziness, one-half craziness, or three-quarters craziness. All the religions and races have three-quarters craziness.

All the astrology and horoscopes have three-quarters craziness. Their research has from one-quarter to three-quarters craziness. Those who have one-quarter craziness have a specific kind of craziness and a specific kind of sorrow, those who have one-half craziness have a heavier sorrow, and those who have three-quarter craziness have an even greater sorrow, the sorrow of enmity and hatred. As the craziness grows, the heaviness of the sorrow grows. But when full craziness comes, when full wisdom comes, there is no craziness; peace and tranquility come.

If one has one-quarter wisdom, he will know suffering. With one-half wisdom, he will know more suffering; there will be both happiness and sorrow. If he has three-quarters wisdom, he will have even more suffering and even more difficulties. But if full wisdom comes, he will have no craziness. There will be complete tranquility, everything will be understood. That will be peace. There will be no differences of religion, race, scriptures, and philosophies. There will only be one point. One family, one point, one God, one prayer, and one life—this is what he will know. Until that (full wisdom) comes, he will be crazy.

The other crazinesses are also like this. All the crazinesses will come. But (if full wisdom comes), there is one God, one family, one section, one prayer. Everything is his own life—his life, his soul—one truth. He understands that everything exists within him. Whatever desire, whatever sorrow, whatever suffering exists, it is within him. He understands this. Then he can learn, "Oh, this part is wrong, this part is right, this part is correct," and he can repair the motor. With wisdom, he can repair the motor that runs his life and the motor that runs his mind, the world motor: "This is the mind, and that is life, the soul motor," and he will have peace. This is psychology, this is the *secret soul*. This is the *secret soul psychology* of life.

The soul is an example. The five elements of earth, fire, water, air, and ether, or maya, are examples that are *rounding* inside and outside. Earth, fire, water, and air are inside and earth, fire, water, and air are outside—rounding. This is the world. The other is the soul world, the life world. One is the physical world, the *dunyā*, of the five elements. That (other) is the life world, the life world of the soul. We need to understand these. When we understand them, we can repair them.

It is the thoughts that must be changed. It is the thoughts that are crazy. Every section is crazy. Illness, disease, sorrow, and suffering must be changed. If we can keep on changing each of these sections, then truth will grow, and happiness and peace will develop. As long as we do not cut these, one by one, sorrows, difficulties, separations, divisions, enmity, and differences will grow. The things that come must be cut, one by one. As thoughts arise in the mind, they must be cut. That is wisdom psychology. That is God's psychology. To cut, with wisdom, each emotion as it arises in the mind is creation's secret psychology. We have to search for the wisdom to do this.

My love you, my children, my sons, my daughters, my grandsons, granddaughters, brothers, and sisters. Each one of us must think of this. It is easy to speak about this, but it is difficult to understand. Understanding this is psychology. The correct treatment is to give medicine to our own lives. One who can provide the medicine to cure these illnesses is a good doctor. He is a good psychologist, a good doctor, a good teacher, a good *gnāni*. He is an Insān Kāmil, a good man. He is God's son. He is a *truth man*. We should think of this. If we know this and finish this work properly, *shari,* that is good. That is peace, tranquility, equality, equanimity, unity, one lineage, one God, and one family.

All the time we do not understand this, we will be sad. We

will have divisions, separations, murder, sin, the differences of "I" and "you," torpor, bile, and craziness. All of these will be there. We need to think about this, my sons, my daughters. Please understand this. This is wisdom. Psychology is the clarity of wisdom, the understanding of how to remove our illness, the illness of our birth. This is the study that cuts away our sorrow and suffering. This is the learning that ends our worries and eliminates our differences. This is a secret, the secret of man-God, *man-God secret. Happy.* If we understand and learn this, we will be happy, we will always be happy, we will be happy every day. *Every day, one God, pray.* We should think of this. My love you.

If wisdom comes, if it comes to you in its completeness, then that is the fulfillment of your life. Just as the flower and fragrance are joined together, when truth, which is a secret, joins with your life, it will have a fragrance within it—God. That Light, that fragrance, that plenitude, and that happiness will be there. That is peace. God's grace, God's treasure, God's kingdom, God's wealth and beauty will all come within you. His qualities and actions, everything will come. Tranquility will come. That is the fragrance of God—Light.

What else is needed? That is heaven, that is the kingdom of God, that is happiness, that is your wealth, the wealth of peace. That is the secret life, secret God, secret heaven, and secret happiness. You will see happiness, heaven, and God within you. But you must understand it correctly. Without understanding, if you have one-quarter craziness, one-half craziness, or three-quarter craziness, as long as you have that craziness—you will not have peace.

You need to fully join one side or the other. Either fully join the crazy side of the world, the side of maya, and be immersed in hell—"All right, go!" or fully join the side of wisdom—God, heaven. If you are fully crazy on the side of the world, and run here and there, or are happy or sad, or take off your clothes, you will be unaware of anything. You will not know anything. Rice and feces will be the same to you; good and bad will be the same to you; joy and sorrow will be the same to you. But if you go on this (other) path, you will keep cutting away everything. You will cut what is wrong, you will cut the thoughts of the mind. God's Point is there. That is full peace. Wherever you are will be the kingdom of God. You will be in the kingdom of God here. That is heaven. You will see Him, you will see that fragrance, that Light, that plenitude, that happiness, and that unity. Please understand this.

My love you. Every male and female, every human being should understand this in his life. *Gnānam* learning, guru learning, mantra learning, and tricks learning is for self-business, for the sake of the one-span stomach. When hunger comes, the ten (commandments) will fly away. We must know this. My love you.

Ah *shari*. This wisdom must come if we are to research into God. With this wisdom we can understand about Him, about our Father, about what His Power is like. We can know more about His Power. Once this true wisdom comes to you, you must analyze yourself. You must analyze your life—the soul, the pure soul. You should understand this. Who is this (soul)? What is this soul? What kind of thing is it? Where did it come from? What is its state? Which is its house? Where is it? This is not something that can be seen by earth, fire, water, air, mind, and desire. They cannot see it. The earth, the air, the water, and the fire that are in the body do not know it. Illusion does not know it. The archangels, Jibrīl, Mīkā'īl, Isrāfīl, and 'Izrā'īl, may the peace of God be upon them, do not know it. The *malaks*, angels, the *malā'ikat*, archangels, and the *nabīmārgal,* prophets, do not know it.

Where does it come from? The Sound comes, the Light comes, the *Mulakkam,* Resonance comes, the *Wahy,* the Sound or Revelation comes, the Fragrance comes, the Rays come, and the Explanation comes. Where are they coming from? The soul came. From where did it come? Where is it coming from? Each Point is coming. On the path of the Point that is coming, you cannot place an *opposite* in its way. That Point will break apart anything that comes in its way; it will stop everything....*stop, stop, stop.* Whatever you place in front of it, it will *stop, stop.* If you try to make something equal to it, it will break it. It breaks apart everything else. It is a great weapon that splits apart and reveals everything in creation. It explains everything. It is a Power. It is God.

Where is this coming from? You must cut the soul with divine luminous wisdom, *pahut arivu,*[1] *Qutbiyyat arivu,*[2] *pērarivu, Nūr arivu*[3] and *gnāna arivu.*[4] We have to cut that soul and look. We have to keep cutting to find out where this Truth is coming from.

Cut one particle and look.
What is the value of that Power?
What is it like?

With this wisdom, take hold of that Power.
Take one particle and cut that particle with wisdom.

---

1. *pahut arivu* (T) Divine analytic wisdom, the sixth of the seven levels of wisdom
2. *Qutbiyyat arivu* (A & T) Divine analytic wisdom; the wisdom of the Qutb ☉, the wisdom that explains the truth of God.
3. *Nūr arivu* (A & T) The wisdom of the *Nūr,* which is Light; divine luminous wisdom.
4. *gnāna arivu* (T) Grace-awakened wisdom.

From that Power, take one particle, one ray, one soul-ray.
From those rays of wisdom, the rays of the *Nūr*, the Light,
take one ray, cut it with that wisdom, and look.
That is God's Power.

Out of ten million pieces, take one atom, one ray, and, with the
wisdom of the *Nūr*, the Light, that Plenitude, cut that ray into
a billion parts, and look.
Having cut it, take one part and look at it through *pērarivu,*
divine luminous wisdom, that microscope.

If you look at that one part, you will see ninety-nine, ninety-
nine, ninety-nine,
tonnūru onbathu, tonnūru onbathu, tonnūru onbathu,
revolving around and around, one without touching the other,
one without touching the other.
Ninety-nine, ninety-nine are revolving around each other
without touching.
Ninety-nine, ninety-nine, ninety-nine,
rotating one without touching the other.
Ahhh.

Take that particle and cut it further into a hundred million
parts. Look.
Take one of those parts and look.
Within that, you will see one revolving around the other
without touching,
one revolving around the other without touching,
with an even greater power,
an even greater power.

The rays are more intense, the power is more intense,
the *lightning* is greater.
They are revolving, ninety-nine, ninety-nine, one around the
other without touching.
Oooh.
The eyes cannot see,
The outer eye cannot see.
Ooooh.

Take one particle and cut it into ten million parts,
Take one particle and look,
look at it subtly.
In that particle, you will see ninety-nine, ninety-nine revolving
round and round,
one without touching the other.
That has more power.
That power, that lightning, that ray is even greater.

Take that particle and cut it into five million pieces
and look at it.
If you cut that and look at one particle,
you will see ninety-nine, ninety-nine, ninety-nine
revolving around each other without touching.
It has even more power.
The power is so strong that it is pulling you in.
It has the power to pull in your soul, you, and your wisdom.
The magnet is pulling, pulling, pulling…
particle, particle.

Take that (particle) and cut it into twenty-five thousand pieces

and again look at one part.
You will find (ninety-nine, ninety-nine) revolving around
each other without touching,
and that power is even greater.
Ahhh!

You are unable to look deeply.
The pull is very strong, drawing you in, drawing you in.
Oooh, oooh, oooh.
What a *pudinam,* what a wonder!
It is drawing in your mind and your essence.
It is drawing in your life,
drawing it in,
drawing it in.

Cut that (one particle) into twelve thousand particles.
Take one part and look.
Then cut that into ten thousand,
then cut that into five thousand,
then cut that into three thousand,
then cut that into one thousand,
then cut that into ninety-nine pieces,
and take one of those parts and look.
You are not aware of yourself,
you are absorbed,
gone, *vilinta poit*—
one (revolving) around the other without touching,
one without touching the other.
You are absorbed into that Light, that Power.

You are gone,

poit.

You are unable to do any further analysis because you are
no longer there.
You have been absorbed.

That Power keeps on revolving without one touching the other. No matter how many parts you cut—using all that you have
learned in your life, in the world, and in all of everything—you
cannot analyze even the smallest part of that Power, one tiny ray,
one *atom ray.* You cannot analyze one atom ray of the full Power
of God's history. Not one atom. Before you can analyze one ray of
His *sifāt,* creation, His *dhāt,* essence, His actions, conduct, and His
ninety-nine *wilāyats,* attributes, before you can analyze one ray of
His Power, before you can finish this, you will be gone; you will
disappear, be drawn in. We can never fully analyze or know what
such a Power is like, how great is this Power—God—the soul!

If you take one ray of your life and subtly analyze and look at
it with wisdom, (you will see) ninety-nine, ninety-nine. As you go
on looking, you will see ninety-nine, ninety-nine revolving, one
without touching the other. This state that we are talking about
is the history of one atom, the research into one ray. With this
form (of ours), we cannot fully analyze and see It. Only if you go
beyond that (form) and research, can you analyze It. Only if you
disappear within It can you understand about It. That is God,
God's Truth, that Power. That is Āndavan, Kadavul, God, Allāh,
one Point. That is ruling (everything). You must reflect on this.

This is analyzed within. Whatever you study and investigate
within yourself is psychology. Whatever medicine you research
into, its qualities and actions, that is psychology. Wisdom, studies,

attachments, whatever you touch in order to understand yourself is psychology. Whatever sorrow and distress you see within yourself must be analyzed and cut away. That is psychology. You must cut away whatever illness, disease, mind, desire, thought, or craziness that appears in you. Analyze and cut away whatever separations, happiness, differences, sorrows, and troubles that come within you, using the weapons of wisdom, faith, *īmān*, certitude, and determination. There are seven different wisdoms. You must cut (whatever comes) with *madi*, judgment, *nuparivu*, subtle wisdom, *pahut arivu*, divine analytic wisdom, and *pērarivu*, divine luminous wisdom. Cut each thing with the *pahut arivu* of the *Qutbiyyat*, the explaining wisdom, *gnāna* wisdom. To cut away and clear whatever comes in your life is psychology. You must understand what is within you; you need to know what is inside you. Whatever is wrong, cut it. Whatever causes you sadness, cut it. Whatever causes you sorrow, cut it. This is psychology. This is our medicine. This is the treatment we must give ourselves.

Whatever thought causes suffering, cut it. Whatever causes enmity, cut it. Whatever causes hostility, cut it. Whatever causes doubt, cut it. Whatever causes suspicion, cut it. Whatever self-business comes, cut it. When *love, moham,* comes, cut it. When duality comes, cut it. To cut these within ourselves is psychology.

This is the treatment that will cure our illness. This is what each one of us must do. We have to cut everything, every *body,* every emotion in order to cure our illness. This is the reason we need wisdom. We need wisdom, faith, certitude, and determination to cut these. We must find a (true) Shaikh of wisdom, a wise man, a man with clear wisdom to show us the way of our state. Do not wander in search of *gnānam,* divine wisdom. Do not search for a guru or a mantra. Do not search for magics, mantras, supernatural powers, or miracles.

The disease lives within you:

arrogance, karma, and maya,
tārahan, singhan, and *sūran,* the three sons of maya,
desire, anger, miserliness, attachment, fanaticism, and envy,
intoxicants, lust, theft, murder, and falsehood,
earth, fire, water, and air,
desire for earth, desire for woman, and desire for gold,
separations of race, religion, scriptures, and philosophies,
the sixty-four sexual games and the sixty-four arts and sciences,
all the dancing and singing, all the differences,
hunger, disease, old age, and death,
hastiness and impatience,
the arrogance of the "I" and the pride of "mine,"
jealousy, falsehood, differences of "I" and "you," and anger.

Hastiness is the enemy of wisdom. Impatience will eat up wisdom. Anger is the guru of sin. Lust is greater than the ocean. (But) one who does duty, realizing the truth, will receive the plenitude of the grace of God—that is a great gift.

Like this, there are four hundred trillion illnesses within you. These are karmic diseases. When you are keeping these illnesses within you, why do you search for miracles, wisdom, occult powers, mantras, and prayer? You will fall down if you have these illnesses. If you go on your journey with these illnesses, you will fall down. If you fall down and curl up at each place, how can you proceed? You cannot travel with these illnesses. They are killing you.

You must search for the wisdom to remove these illnesses. You need the wisdom, the qualities, that knowledge, and the actions to cure these illnesses. You have to find a man of wisdom, an Insān Kāmil, to open the path and cut these diseases. Only when you get rid of this illness will you be able to get up and proceed. This disease that is killing you is inside you. It is a fatal disease that is born with you. It was born with your body, and is killing you and causing you to suffer. You are carrying the disease that is making you suffer.

When a Shaikh comes, when a Guru, a Shaikh of wisdom, an Insān Kāmil comes and tries to cut this disease, it hurts you. It causes you suffering. My love you, my children. The disease that is born with you is killing you. That disease is murdering you. When an Insān Kāmil comes to kill that murderous illness that is born with you, when he comes to cut the jealousy disease, the envy disease, the lust disease, the love disease, the sex disease, the color disease, the race disease, the religion disease, the scripture disease, the philosophy disease, the mantra disease, the tantra disease, the tricks disease, the hunger disease, the old age disease, the death disease, you say, "Hey, he has cut these! *Aiyō,* oh no, he has cut my love, *aiyoooo,* this swamiyar has done this to me! He has cut my alcohol, he has cut my marijuana. He is a crazy man! Ooh! I am suffering! He has cut my desire!"

Every time he cuts you, it is painful. When your mind is cut, you feel pain and cry, "Oooooh." Then you leave him and run away. When your illness is cut, it hurts, so you run away with your illness. *Running, running.* You take your illness with you, and run. Then what can he do? He is cutting off what is causing you pain, but you run away, shouting, "He is cutting my ears, cutting my eyes, cutting my hunger, cutting my nose. Ooh, he is hurting me!"

He is cutting the disease that is born with you. This disease is born with you and is killing you, but if he cuts it, you run. Then he says, "*Shari, shari, po,* all right, all right, go. Go, do what you like."

The teachings of wisdom that are given to you go between two mountains; the sound echoes between love and illusion, between the mind and the sexual arts. The sound echoes between the two mountains. You are standing in between these two mountains and when you call out, "*Aiyō,* come, come, come here," the sound returns as, "Oh, come, come." It calls to you. When you shout, "Go, go," it echoes back, as "Go, go." "Come, come," calls you, "Come, come." When he calls you to "Come here," to come to his place, you reply, "Come here, come, come to my place." You are in between the two mountains, calling others to come to your place, "Come here" or "Go, go—go, go, you go." This is what you are doing.

When I try to cut, you get angry. You are always in this state. Every thought in every mind is like this. No one can cut it, because you will run. You need a true man to cut it. A wise Shaikh must cut it in order to save you. He must cut your karmic disease in order to save you. If it hurts you, what can he do? What can he do? He says, "Thank you, go and do what you like. *Shari po,* go and analyze this later. Go!" and he lets you go. He tries as much as he can and then lets you go, and says, "All right, go." He says, "Nothing can be done through my actions. He (God) has to do it." He says, "O God, there is nothing that I can do. Each one has to look after his own actions. What can I do?"

This is what an Insān Kāmil does. This is psychology, the inner secret study. This is the way that illnesses are cut away and sorrows are dispelled. This is the way to know God. This is the truth. We have to understand this, my children, grandsons, granddaughters, my sons, my daughters, children, brothers, and sisters. You need to think a little about this.

This is psychology. This is *God-man psychology*. This is today's study of God-man psychology, the study of truth, of life. Please think of this. *Āmīn. Al-hamdu lillāh.* All praise is to Allāh.

Now, today, the study of psychology is finished, *mudi.* This is what you should understand, this is what you need to know. *Āmīn. Al-hamdu lillāh. As-salāmu 'alaikum wa rahmatullāhi wa barakātuhu.* May the peace, the beneficence, and the blessings of God be upon you. This study is finished.

A'ūdhu billāhi minash-shaitānir-rajīm.
I seek refuge in God from the accursed satan.

Bismillāhir-Rahmānir-Rahīm.
In the name of God, the Most Compassionate, the Most Merciful.

The Only True Psychology Is the Purity of Islām

March 16, 1982, Tuesday 9:30 AM

My children, grandsons, granddaughters, my sons, my daughters, my sisters and brothers, my love you. Earlier we spoke about psychology. We finished that talk about God. Now let us speak about its basis, its foundation, *ātāram*.

> There is one Father: the Great Father, *Paramapidā*.
> There is one family: the family of man, the *creation family*,
> the society of man. There is one God: Allāh, Āndavan,
> the One who is formless, a Power.
> There is one prayer: God. That Power is prayer.

There is one family, and there are also countless families, countless creations, limitless, limitless creations. There are sea creations, land creations, jungle creations, city creations, earth creations, fire creations, water creations, air creations, and ether creations. There is the sun, the moon, and the stars. There are creations that can be seen by the eyes and creations that cannot be seen by the eyes. There are trees, weeds, grass, gems, gold, jewels, silver, mercury, and chemicals. God has created innumerable creations like this, and He has also created the one family

175

that can understand these creations. There is one family that can understand and know all of these. That family is known as man, the human being.

All the angels, *malaks,* the archangels, *malā'ikat,* the light beings, *olimārgal,* the jinns, fairies, heavenly beings, ghosts, satans, and the five elements have been created with thirty-six *tattwas,* powers. Man has ninety-six *tattwas.* Man, who has these ninety-six *tattwas,* is His (God's) representative, His son. He does His duty. Man is the one who has been created in the form that can do His duty. The life of man is purity, *suwādarnam*[1]—peace and purity. His whole life is purity, cleanliness; throughout his entire life he understands purity. His way is to know and understand all lives. It is to this exalted man alone that this knowledge is given.

God is the Creator of all creations. Our Father is the Father for all lives. He has created and brought to life every creation—from the atom, the two-legged and four-legged beings, beings that have no legs and beings that have legs, beings that live eating earth, beings that live breathing air, beings that live eating weeds and grass, those that live eating leaves, from those that live eating bad things to those that live eating good things. In water, there are those that live eating what is discarded and those that live eating what is good. There are those that live eating fruit and there are those that live on the essence of the fruit.

Like this, for the countless beings that He has created, He has also created their different foods. There are some beings that eat flowers, others that extract the essence or honey, and others that take the pollen. Some insects and bugs take the essence of gold and live on that and some eat the earth itself and live on that. Some (beings) eat light and live on that and some eat darkness and live

---

1. *suwādarnam* (T) Purity, health, cleanliness.

on that. Some take the truth and live on that and some take evil and live on that. God has created many creations like this.

God, our Father, has created all of these, and has given wisdom to man so he can understand creation in its entirety. Our Father understands the point that He has placed within these creations, and according to their nature, provides the food that is necessary for them. For those that eat the leaf, He has created the leaf. For those that drink the juice of the leaf, He has given the juice. For those that eat fruit, He has given the fruit, and for those that draw the essence from the fruit, He has placed the essence inside it. For those that eat seeds, there is the seed, and for those that eat the essence of the seed, He has placed the essence inside the seed. For those that drink water, there is water, and for those that eat the chemical that is inside water, there is the chemical. For those that eat fire, there is fire, and for those that live on the heat of the fire, there is heat. For those that live on air, there is air, and for those that breathe the oxygen from the air, He has given the oxygen.

Like this, when He created each being, when He gave form to each being, He created their actions, their qualities, and their food. He did this for every creation. Our Father, who created these beings, has given us the wisdom to understand them. From the grass, from the trees, from the weeds, from the atoms, from the animals, from the sun, from the moon, from the stars, from man, from the reptiles, from the ants, from the water and the air, we should understand these. They do not (all) talk. There are beings that talk and beings that do not talk. There are many tens of millions of languages. He knows all the languages that He created. What is the language? It is the language that He has given.

God, our Father, has the heart, the clear heart, the truth-mind, the truth-wisdom that is the magnet that can pull in and understand every creation. It is a compass. The compass sees, understands, and acts accordingly. It is a television. He uses that truth, that television, that light, that nature, that judgment, that justice, and those beautiful qualities. It is with these that He acts; this is how He understands. This is His psychology.

He looks at their aspect and does what is needed for that section. He gives them peace. He can see everything—their form, their look, their thoughts, their yearning, and their intention. Upon seeing this, He does (what is right) for that point. He is the mirror for all lives. When they come in front of Him, everything can be seen and cleared. He does not question them, He does not talk to them, He does not ask them how things are. He immediately understands that point, that sound, that explanation, that resonance—the sound of the mind, the sound of the soul, and the sound of the five elements. He understands what the right section is for them, and gives it.

Like this, He does this for the creations that move and do not move, for the creations of the ocean, the creations of the land, the creations of the jungle, the particle creations, the atom creations, the demon creations, the jinns, fairies, angels, archangels, man, and animals. God—this is His psychology. This psychology is purity. Whatever He does is pure. A pure life is: His unity, equality, peace, equanimity, tranquility, and serenity, it is peace and tranquility in life. This is psychology, the psychology He does.

God has given this psychology to us. He has given man ninety-six *tattwas,* powers. He has given the pure soul—the *mīm*—Muhammad ☉. He has given *lām*—the Light, the wisdom of *gnānam.* He has given the power of *alif*—God, His truth, His plenitude. Out of one hundred, *nūr,* He has given man ninety-six and three, ninety-nine. He has given ninety-nine powers, *tattwas,* to man. Having given these ninety-nine, He rules with the one Power which is Truth. God, the Father—that is Truth. Having given ninety-nine (to man), He rules with that Truth, that Power. That is God, Allāh. He has given us these *tattwas* in totality. These explanations are our psychology. They show us what we should do.

Only a man can bring about the purity where all beings can live in peace, equality, and tranquility. Only a son-God, a son, can do God's work. The son alone is a human being. Man is God's son, he is a human being. Adam ☻ is the son of God, and man is the son of Adam ☻ and Hawwa' (Eve) ☻. Man is known as Adam; human beings are the children of God.

To understand every being and to give them peace is purity. The purity of life is the explanation of man's psychology. This is psychology; to give purity and peace to every life is man's psychology. We must understand this, we must do this, we must know this, and we must give this.

The earth is an open space and the sky is an open space. This is round, a circle, an open space. All of His creations are found in this open space—the sun, the moon, the stars, those with form and those without form, air, water, fire, earth, satan, sounds, forces, creations, light, darkness, thunder, and lightning. All of these can be understood in the two sections of the earth-world and the sky-world. What will he (man) understand in these two sections? Using the ninety-nine powers, *tattwas,* he will understand purity, the purity of life.

Heaven and hell. Is hell pure or is heaven pure? Is life pure? Which has peace, which has tranquility? This needs to be understood. Understanding this in life is purity. To know the way to understand all lives, and to act accordingly, is purity. This is psychology. Man should give peace, equality, and tranquility to all lives. The understanding of unity, harmony, and the one family is purity, the peace and purity of life. If there are any differences in a man's life, it is not purity. This will cause both suffering and sorrow. When differences come, his purity will leave. Purity is destroyed by (the divisions of) land, countries, cities, and languages. Earth, woman, gold, wealth, differences of "mine" and "yours," and languages destroy his purity. These kill the purity in other lives; they create separations, differences, fighting, and quarrels. These are not pure. The purity of life is unity. The purity of life is harmony. The purity of life is truth. The purity of life is goodness, truth, tranquility, and peace.

To find peace and tranquility in oneself, and thereby see peace and tranquility in others is psychology. You need to understand this. What you are learning is not psychology. The life of man is psychology. When we understand the way God understands, and when we complete our work with the use of the ninety-nine powers, *kāranangal,* that is psychology. This is called Islām. Islām is purity, it is psychology.

Islām came as a final proof from God. God sent each of the prophets: Ādam, Nūh, Ibrāhīm, Ismāʿīl, Mūsā, Dāwūd, ʿĪsā, Muhammad, Idrīs, Ishāq, Ayyūb, Yaʿqūb, Sālih, Yūsuf, Sulaimān,[2] may the peace of God be upon them all. God sent down these prophets for every section. He sent Muhammad ⊕ as the final prophet to teach about this purity. This is psychology, this is purity. What is known as Islām is purity. This purity is the psychology where one heart understands the other heart, where one mind understands the other mind and gives peace, where one thought understands the other thought and gives love, and where one body embraces the other body and shows it love and compassion. Each person in each house embraces with love. Each body

---

2. These are among the twenty-five prophets mentioned in the Qurʾān. In the text, their names are given in Arabic. The English equivalents are: Adam, Noah, Abraham, Ishmael, Moses, David, Jesus, Muhammad, Idris, Isaac, Job, Jacob, Salih, Joseph, and Solomon, may the peace of God be upon them all.

unites with the other's body, each heart unites with the other's heart and embraces with love. The illness of life, the illness of the body, the illness of demons, the illness of sorrow, the illness of worry, the illness of poverty, the illness of disease, the illness of hunger, the illness of old age, and the illness of death should be understood by everyone. We must embrace others, cure these illnesses, and give peace.

Peace, unity, and equality....when we are in one place, when we live in one place, eat in one place, sleep in one place, disappear in one place, die in one place, when our final judgment is given in one place, and when we finally join together in heaven in one place, that is unity. Even when we go to that (final) place, we all live together in freedom as one family, one group. In this world and in the next world we live together in freedom, as one family of peace. This is Islām. If we find this way of peace, this is Islām. Where is peace and purity? Purity is found in one's life and in one's body. That will be a life without illness. Every child should realize a life free of illness.

Does Islām fight over land? No. Islām does not fight over land. Does it fight over politics, or does it fight over religion, or does it fight over race, or does it fight over gold or wealth, does it fight about separations, does it fight about divisions, does it fight about color? No. It has one Point—Truth—God, Truth, one Father, and one family.

We must accept the Father. We must know the One who nourishes, sustains, and protects us. We must accept Him as our Father. To live a life without ignorance, to realize purity, to know our life, and to know our Father is purity for our lives. When the Father and the children join together in one place, that is heaven, that is love. One unity, one family, one Father, one prayer, one Truth—that is heaven. To be of one lineage, with one Father, to pray to the One, to exist as one family in hunger, illness, old age, happiness, and sorrow, to understand and help one another, and to know the purity of the soul, is Islām.

Know the purity of life. Understand what is clean and what is unclean, and then you will be clean and pure and have peace and tranquility. When one has a connection to his Father, when he is in a state where he knows his Father, when he reaches the state where he prays to Him, he will understand that there is one blood, one lineage, one body, one family, one mind, one sorrow, one life, one soul, and one food. This is the purity of life, and this is Islām. This is what God speaks about. Islām is this.

Fighting and arguing is not Islām. There is one Father; that is Allāhu *akbar*. We say, "Allāh is the great One. Allāh is the great One." To kill one another is not Islām. Allāhu *akbar*, Allāh is the great One. Do not destroy someone who is evil, but destroy what is evil (within yourself) and reap what is good. To destroy darkness and create light is purity. To destroy the evil quality and create the good quality is purity. To destroy the bad food and create the good food is purity. Purity is: to destroy the bad action and create the good action, to destroy bad speech and create good speech, to destroy bad sight and create good sight, to destroy bad smells and create good fragrances, to cut away bad sounds and hear good sounds, to destroy a bad life and create a good life, to destroy the bad path and go on the good path, to cut off accepting bad things and accept the good things from God, to cut away bad thoughts and accept good thoughts, to cut away differences and divisions and have unity, to give up anger and have patience and peacefulness, to cut away arrogance, karma, and maya, illusion, and take *alif, lām,* and *mīm*—the pure soul, wisdom, and God. Give up arrogance, karma, and maya and join with the soul, wisdom, and God, the good qualities.

Give up selfishness, have equality, and treat all lives as your own life. Purify your qualities and give this purity to others. The purity of one's life is Islām. This is purity.

Islām is purity, psychology:
One knows the other and helps him.
One knows the hunger of the other and helps him.
One knows the sorrow of the other and helps him.
One knows the sadness of the other and helps him.
One knows who has hunger, illness, old age,
and death and gives him assistance.

Knowing death, say,
"Allāhu *akbar*.
Lā ilāha illAllāh,
Muhammadur-Rasūlullāh.
Innā lillāhi wa innā ilaihi rāji'ūn.
God is great.
Other than God nothing exists. Only You are God,
Muhammad is the Messenger of God.
Truly we belong to God and are returning to Him."

"God created you, God is calling you back. Your Father is calling you back. My brother, you came from God and now your Father is calling you back. You go ahead, I will follow. There is no separation between us, there is no separation in *dunyā*, this world, or in *ākhirah*, His kingdom. There is no separation in our lives. There might have been a little (coming and) going in our journeys, but there is no separation in our hearts. In this kingdom there is no separation, there is unity. In our Father's kingdom, there is no separation. That is Islām. There is no dying. According to this purity, we have no death. According to this purity and unity, we do not die. *Dying no!* The Father has called you first, so you must go. I will follow later. I will finish my duty, and then come. There is no death. We are always there." This is purity, psychology. It is this unity that is Islām. This is what the Rasūl, Prophet Muhammad ⊕ was told by God.

Islām is to know unity. Money, land, swords, fights, and separations are not Islām. Unity is Islām, love is Islām, compassion is Islām, patience is Islām, peace is Islām, equality is Islām, tranquility is Islām. This is psychology. Knowing each heart and helping each according to its needs is Islām. To be without sorrow and to have equality and peace is Islām, peace. This is what God calls Islām.

Capturing lands, cities, countries, and territories is not Islām. To accept Allāh is Islām. Allāh has said that you should accept your Father; Allāh has said that you should accept and know your Father. "You are His children, accept Him." This is what He has said.

The fight is against ignorance, lack of wisdom, and arrogance. In that fight you say, "Allāhu *akbar*, Allāh is the great One," and you are the one who is destroyed. Your desire, arrogance, fanaticism, jealousy, envy, the "I" and "you" are destroyed.

"Allāhu *akbar*, Allāh is the great One."
You are annihilated.
"Allāh is the great One. Allāhu *akbar*."
You are destroyed.

Every time you fall down, say,
"Allāhu *akbar*."

When your arrogance is dying, say, "Allāhu *akbar.*" Your arrogance is dying, your separations are dying, your craziness is dying, your ignorance is dying, your karma is dying. Satan who was inside you is dying. Jealousy, envy, deceit, bad qualities, and the four hundred trillion, ten thousand spiritual qualities are dying, this is what is dying. When you are dying, you do not say, "I am the greatest one!" You say "Allāhu *akbar,* Allāh is the great One, Allāh is great!"

The sun, moon, and stars will one day perish, they will all disappear. They are not great ones. The earth, sky, world, and nether world are not great ones. Allāh is the great One. Allāh, Allāh—that Point, that Truth is the greatest. Understand this Allāhu *akbar.*

Islām is unity and equality. Understanding this is psychology. To understand that in each *qalb* there is nothing other than one truth, one unity, one faith, and one prayer—that peace, unity, compassion, and equality—is purity of life. There is nothing else. This is purity. The purity of life is freedom. There is no other purity. This is the purity of life.

We must know this, we must do this, and we must act on this. Everything else is evil and will perish. This unity is Islām, this one point is Islām, this one section is Islām, this research is Islām, this psychology is Islām, this purity is Islām, this love is Islām. This is what is called Islām. We must understand this.

While we are alive, when we are born, and when we die there are no separations. Here and there we are joined together, in the same place. We eat in the same place, we live in the same place, we disappear in the same place, we die in the same place, and we again join together and live with our Father in the same place.

Goodness is Islām. Truth is Islām. Fighting for the sake of capturing lands and cities, or for the sake of languages is not Islām.

To have faith in the one Father, to worship the one Father, and to accept the one Father is Islām, where the children of Adam ☺ join together as one family, one human race, and one lineage, and treat all lives as their own life, giving peace to them. This unity is Islām. To have no hatred is Islām, to have no divisions is Islām, to have no separations is Islām. Compassion is Islām, patience is Islām, peace, tranquility, and purity are Islām. This is the purity of life. The purity of a life without illness is Islām. This state is Islām, purity, psychology. This is the lesson one learns within himself.

The purity of Islām is to study, understand, and know God, our Father, on the outside and the inside. This is what we must understand. Understanding this is Islām. If we can cause this to happen in ourselves, that is Islām, and we will be able to give peace to all lives. The family that gives peace to all lives is Islām. Dispelling birth, karma, and illness, and giving peace to all lives is Islām. One who understands what Islām is, is Islām. If he knows the unity of prayer and peace, if he knows the unity of praying together in one congregation, then he is Islām.

One who understands the human society, and knows it as one family, the children of Adam ☺, is a *mu'min*, a true believer, a pure man. That is psychology, purity. If he understands that all lives are one, if he understands that there is one Father, one prayer, and one family, then he is *mu'maiana* Islām, he is a *mu'min*, he is Islām. We must understand this. This is purity. This is psychology, the learning that understands the self.

God has studied Himself and has understood everything within Himself. He has cut away evil and dwells in goodness. Like this, to understand everything, to cut away evil, to dwell in goodness, and to find peace there, is psychology. That is Islām. Acting in this way is peace. May we think of this. *Āmīn.* May each and every child think about what Islām is. *Āmīn. Āmīn.* This is psychology.

Finally, God showed the Rasūl ⊕ what Islām is. You need to understand this. If you understand it, that is the Qur'ān. The *wahys*, revelations, the 6,666 *āyats*, verses, have been sent down to you and are within you. All the hadith have been sent down and are placed within you. The ninety-nine *wilāyats*, attributes, are placed within you. All His actions are placed within you, all the *wahys* are within you. You must speak with that. If you want to understand that, you must establish the state of purity. You will only be able to understand and speak to it when you understand equality, peace, equanimity, and tranquility. Understanding and studying this within ourselves is psychology; it is purity. If you understand this you are pure. If you do not understand this, you are impure, and there is no purity in your life.

As long as you do not understand this, there is no purity in your life. There is no freedom or purity. A man who does not understand this will have no purity. He will have no happiness, no peace, no equality, and no tranquility in his life. He will not have serenity or peace in the two worlds, even for one second.

It is only after he understands this that he will have peace, tranquility, equality, unity, and harmony and know that there is one family, one race. He must receive this and find peace.

This is psychology. This is what we must study. *Āmīn.*

Glossary

The following traditional honorific phrases in Arabic calligraphy are used in the text:

- ﷺ *sallAllāhu 'alaihi wa sallam,* may Allāh bless him and grant him peace, is used after mentioning the name of Prophet Muhammad, the Rasūlullāh, the Messenger of Allāh.

- ﷐ *'alaihis-salām,* peace be upon him, is used after mentioning the name of a prophet, messenger, or angel.

- ﷜ *radiyAllāhu 'anhu* or *'anhā,* may Allāh be pleased with him or her, is used after mentioning the name of a companion of the Prophet Muhammad ﷐, *Qutbs,* and exalted saints.

- (T) Indicates a Tamil word.

- (A) Indicates an Arabic word.

- (H) Indicates a Hebrew word.

Note: Tamil and Arabic words that have become common usage in the English language are not italicized and those that have not become common usage are italicized. Also, proper names have not been italicized.

For simplicity's sake, we have most often used the English "s" for the plural form of foreign words.

A

adayālam (T) Sign, mark, symbol, representation.

āddu (T) Agitate, dance, shake, wave, move, harass, trouble.

ādi (T) The beginning, primal beginning, source, origin.

aduvai aduvai endru (T) It (God) remains as Itself.

agnānam (T) Ignorance.

Āhāyavani (T) The Hindu god of ether.

aiyō (T) Oh; oh, oh no!

ākhirah (A) More properly *al-ākhirah*. Literally, that which exists after an appointed time. The permanent kingdom of God, comprising both heaven and hell, that exists after the Day of Judgment; the Hereafter. Often contrasted against *ad-dunyā*, this ephemeral world. Belief in *al-ākhirah* is one of the six pillars of faith in Islām. The word appears in the Qur'ān one hundred and fifteen times. (e.g. *Sūratul-Hadīd*, 20th verse: "And in *al-ākhirah* is strong punishment and also forgiveness from Allāh and acceptance.")

Akkinibagavān (T) The Hindu god of fire.

al-hamd (A) The five letters, *alif, lām, mīm, hā', dāl,* of the Arabic alphabet, which constitute the heart. They become transformed in the heart of a true human being into *al-hamd*, the praise of Allāh.

al-hamdu lillāh (A) All praise is to Allāh.

alif (A) The first letter of the Arabic alphabet, equivalent to the English letter "a." To the transformed man of wisdom, *alif* represents Allāh, the One who stands alone.

alif, lām, mīm, hā', dāl (A) Five letters of the Arabic alphabet. They represent the *qalb*, inner heart of man. In the worldly man, hidden within the *hā'* and the *dāl* which correspond to the body of five elements (earth, air, fire, water, and ether) are the *alif*, representing Allāh, the *lām*, representing the *Nūr*, the Light of Allāh or in some usages the revelation of Allāh, and the *mīm* which represents the pure soul, or in some usages the Prophet Muhammad ⊕. When the human being is exalted, the *mīm* splits the *hā'* and the *dāl* and the heart stands as *alif, lām, hā', mīm, dāl* which spells *al-hamd* or praise (of Allāh). In this form the *alif, lām,* and *mīm* are surrounded by the five letters which resplend as the elements transformed into the archangels.

Allāh, Allāhu (A) God.

Allāhu *akbar* (A) God is great.

Allāhu ta'ālā Nāyan (A & T) God Almighty; God is the Highest. Allāhu (A) The beautiful undiminishing One. Ta'ālā (A) The One who exists in all lives in a state of humility and exaltedness. Nāyan (T) The Ruler who protects and sustains.

āmīn (A) So be it.

anādi (T) The beginningless beginning; the state of darkness before creation; the state in which God meditated upon Himself alone; the period of pre-creation when Allāh was alone and unmanifested, unaware of Himself even though everything was within Him; the state before *ādi;* the state of unmanifestation.

anbu (T) Love.

Āndavan (T) God.

ānmā (T) Soul, life.

Ānmā Gnāni (T) A teacher of the soul; one who knows and operates from the soul.

ānma rāchiyam (T) The kingdom of the soul.

ānmā Tahappan (T) The Father of the soul.

ānmā uyir (T) Soul-life.

arivu (T) Wisdom; the fifth of the seven levels of wisdom.

'*arsh* (A) The throne of God; the plenitude from which God rules; the station located on the crown of the head.

arugam pullu (T) A tiny grass that grows in the tropics.

āsai (T) Desire, wish.

as-salāmu 'alaikum wa rahmatullāhi wa barakātahu kulluhu (A) May all the peace, the beneficence, and the blessings of God be upon you.

astaghfirullāhal-'aliyyal-'azīm (A) I ask Allāh, the Exalted and Supreme, for forgiveness.

asura (T) Blood-sucking demon.

ātāram, ātārangal (plural) (T) Basis, foundation, support, security, protection.

a'ūdhu billāhi minash-shaitānir-rajīm (A) I seek refuge in God from the accursed satan.

awwal (A) More properly *al-awwal.* Literally, the *First.* The state in which forms begin to manifest; the beginning of time and space; the stage at which the soul became surrounded by form and each creation took shape; the stage at which the souls of the six kinds of lives (earth life, fire life, water life, air life, ether life, and light life) were placed in their respective forms. Allāh created these forms and then placed that "trust property" which is life within those forms.

āyat (A) A verse in the Qur'ān; a sign or miracle.

B

Bismillāhir-Rahmānir-Rahīm (A) In the name of God, the Most Compassionate, the Most Merciful. *Bismillāh:* Allāh is the first and the last, the One with the beginning and without beginning. He is the One who is the cause for creation and for the absence of creation, the cause for the beginning and for the beginningless. *Ar-Rahmān:* He is the King, the Nourisher, the One who gives food. He is the Compassionate One. He is the One who protects the creations. He is the Beneficent One. *Ar-Rahīm:* He is the One who redeems, the One who protects from evil, who preserves, and who confers eternal bliss; the Savior. On the Day of Judgment and on the Day of Questioning, and on all days from the day of the beginning, He protects and brings His creations back to Himself.

Bismin (A) A shortened form of *Bismillāhir-Rahmānir-Rahīm.*

C

Communaisam (E & T) Bawa Muhaiyaddeen ☻ combines the English word "common" with the Tamil word "*naisam,*" to form the word communaisam—common or equal love for all.

D

dēva rāchiyam (T) The kingdom of God; the kingdom of heaven.

dhāt (A) The essence of God, His treasury, His wealth of purity, His grace.

dunyā (A) The world, the world of physical existence.

G

ganja (T) A selected preparation of marijuana.

gnāna arivu (T) Divine wisdom.

Gnāna Shaikh (A) A spiritual teacher or master who has attained the state of *gnānam,* grace-awakened wisdom. A divinely illumined spiritual guide. One who can point the way to God.

gnānam (T) Divine wisdom; grace-awakened wisdom.

gnāni (T) A wise man; a man of divine wisdom.

Guru (T) The Shaikh; a true Guru; the teacher who awakens the truth within the disciple; the guide who takes the disciple to the shore of the heart; a spiritual teacher.

H

hadith (A) Words of wisdom; discourse of wisdom; story. In Islām, authenticated accounts relating to the deeds and utterances of the Prophet Muhammad ⊕.

halāl (A) Permissible; that which conforms to the commands of God.

harām (A) Impermissible; forbidden; that which does not conform to the commands of God.

hayāt (A) Life; the plenitude of man's eternal life.

hayawān (A) Animal.

hayawān-insān (A) Animal-man.

hurūf (A) Letters.

I

IllAllāhu (A) Only You are Allāh; You alone exist. The second half of the *dhikr, lā ilāha illAllāhu.*

īmān (A) Absolute, complete, and unshakable faith, certitude, and determination that God alone exists; the complete acceptance by the heart that God is One.

*Īmān-*Islām (A) The state of the spotlessly pure heart which contains Allāh's Holy Qur'ān, His divine radiance, His divine wisdom, His truth, His prophets, His angels, and His laws.

When the resplendence of Allāh is seen as the completeness within this pure heart of man, that is *Īmān*-Islām. When the complete unshakable faith of this pure heart is directed towards the One who is completeness and is made to merge with that One, when that heart trusts only in Him and worships only Him, accepting Him as the only perfection and the only One worthy of worship—that is *Īmān*-Islām.

insān (A) Man, a true human being.

insān-hayawān (A) Man-animal.

Insān Kāmil (A) A pure human being or perfected or completed God-realized human being; one who has realized Allāh as his only wealth, cutting away the wealth of the world and the wealth sought by the mind; one who has acquired God's qualities, performs his own actions accordingly, and immerses himself within those qualities; one in whom everything other than Allāh has been extinguished.

Iradchahan (T) God, the Protector.

Islām (A) Purity; unity; the state of total and unconditional surrender to the will of God; the state of absolute purity; to accept the commands of God and His qualities and actions and to establish that state of purity within oneself, worshipping Him alone.

J

jinn (A) A being created from fire.

K

Kadavul (T) God.

kādchi (T) Scene, vision, sight, view, visible appearance.

kalai, kalaigal (plural) (T) The sixty-four arts and sciences acted out in the day, in public, such as music, dance, drama.

kāmil (A) Perfect, perfect one, complete or finished.

Kāmil Shaikh (A) Perfect spiritual guide; the true teacher; the one who, knowing himself and God, guides others on the straight path to Allāh.

karanam, karanangal (plural) (T) Cause, source, origin, principle, essential element, instrument, reason.

kāriyam (T) Effect, result, object, purpose, thing, matter.

karma (T) The inherited qualities formed at the time of conception; the qualities of the essences of the five elements; the qualities of the mind and desire.

kursī (A) The gnostic eye; the eye of Light; the seat of God's knowledge in the center of the forehead where Allāh's *Nūr*, Light, was impressed on the forehead of Adam ☺. Literally, chair, seat, throne.

L

La ilāha illAllāh Muhammadur-Rasūlullāh. Innā lillāhi wa innā ilaihi rāji'ūn (A) Other than God nothing exists. Only You are God. Truly we belong to God and are returning to Him.

lām (A) A letter in the Arabic alphabet, corresponding to the English consonant "l," which stands, within the realm of wisdom, for the *Nūr*, Light, the Light of wisdom.

līlai vinotham (T) The sixty-four sexual games performed at night, in private.

M

madi (T) Judgment, assessment; the fourth of the seven levels of wisdom.

malā'ikat (A) Archangels. Literally, angels.

malak (A) Angel.

mānidan (T) Man, human being.

mantra (T) An incantation or formula; the recitation of a magic word or set of words; sounds imbued with force or energy, through constant repetition, but limited to the energy of the five elements.

manu uyir (T) Human life.

maya (T) Illusion; the unreality of the visible world; the glitters seen in the darkness of illusion.

maya shakti (T) The force of illusion.

mayakkam (T) Torpor, fascination, intoxication, infatuation, stupor, mental delusion.

meygnānam (T) True wisdom.

mīm (A) A letter in the Arabic alphabet, corresponding to the English consonant "m," which stands, within the realm of wisdom, for Muhammad ⊕ or the pure soul.

moham (T) Sensual love, lust.

mudi (T) Finished, completed, ended.

mulakkam (T) Resonance, thunder.

mu'maiana Islām (A & T) A true believer who is Islām, purity.

mu'min (A) A true believer.

N

nabīmārgal (A & T) Prophets.

nadchattiram (T) Star.

nafs, nafs ammārah (A) The seven kinds of base desires, that is, desires meant to satisfy one's own pleasure and comfort. Literally, person, spirit, personality, inclination, or desire which goads or incites one towards evil.

naisam (T) Love.

nallavar (T) A good one.

nānam, nadam, atcham, payirppu (T) The four virtuous qualities of modesty, reserve, shyness, and fear of wrongdoing.

nānūr lacham kōdi (T) Four hundred trillion.

nava kirahangal (T) The nine planets in ancient astrology.

nuparivu (T) Subtle wisdom; the fifth of the seven levels of wisdom.

nuqtah (A) A dot; a dot placed under certain Arabic letters.

Nūr (A) Light; the resplendence of Allāh; the plenitude of the Light of Allāh, which has the resplendence of a hundred million suns; the completeness of Allāh's qualities. When the plenitude of all these becomes One and resplends as One, that is His Light, His *Nūr*. That is Allāh. It is this innate resplendent wisdom that can be awakened in man.

nūr (T) One hundred.

Nūr arivu (A & T) The wisdom of Light.

O

oli (T) Light.

olimārgal (T) Light beings.

oru pidi man (A) One fistful of earth; the heart of man.

P

pahut arivu (T) Divine analytic wisdom; the sixth of the seven levels of wisdom. Muhaiyaddeen ☺. The Wisdom of Allāh that explains His mysteries to the soul. This explanation is the Qur'ān.

panjādcharam (T) A five-lettered incantation; a symbol made of the five Arabic letters: *alif, lām, mīm, hā', and dāl.*

panjāngam (T) Almanac; a book of astrology.

Paramapidā (T) The Great Father, God.

pasi vandal pattum parandu poitch (T) When hunger comes, the ten will fly away. The ten may refer to the Ten Commandments.

pē madam (T) Fecal arrogance; arrogance arising from the anus.

pērarivu (T) Divine luminous wisdom; the seventh of the seven levels of wisdom. God consciousness; awareness that God is One. *Fanā', annihilation in God.*

po (T) Go.

poit (T) Gone.

poitch (T) Finished.

porul (T) Thing, meaning, treasure, reality, truth.

porumai (T) Patience.

poygnānam (T) False wisdom.

pudinam (T) Wonder, miracle.

pullai (T) Child.

purana (T) Literally, an ancient story, a legendary tale or myth. Bawa

Muhaiyaddeen ☺ speaks of the seventeen puranas within man as the qualities of arrogance, karma, and maya, *tārahan, singhan,* and *sūran*—the three sons of maya—desire, anger, miserliness, attachment, fanaticism, envy, intoxicants, lust, theft, murder, and falsehood.

putti (T) Intellect; the third of the seven levels of wisdom.

pytthiam (T) Craziness, obsession, madness, insanity, derangement, delirium, fixation, compulsion.

Q

qalb (A) Heart, the heart within the heart of man, the inner heart. Bawa Muhaiyaddeen ☺ explains that there are two states for the *qalb.* One state is made up of four chambers, which represent Hinduism, Fire Worship, Christianity, and Islām. Inside these four chambers there is a flower, the flower of the *qalb* which is the divine qualities of Allāh. This is the second state, the flower of grace, *rahmat.* God's fragrance exists within this inner *qalb.*

Qur'ān (A) The words of Allāh that were revealed to His Messenger, Prophet Muhammad ☺; those words that came from Allāh's Power are called the Qur'ān; Allāh's inner book of the heart; the Light of Allāh's grace which comes as a resonance from Allāh.

qurbān (A) Inwardly, it is to purify one's heart, *qalb,* by sacrificing and cutting away the animal qualities existing within oneself, thus making one's life *halāl,* permissible. The *subhānallāhi kalimah* is recited for the purpose of destroying these animal qualities within the *qalb.* Outwardly, it is the ritual method for the slaughter of animals to make them *halāl* to eat.

Qutbiyyat (A) The state of divine analytic wisdom, or *pahut arivu,* which is the sixth level of wisdom, the wisdom of the Qutb ☺ that explains the truth of God to the awakened awareness of the human soul.

Qutbiyyat arivu (A & T) The wisdom of the Qutb ☺ that explains the truth of God.

R

Rahīm (A) God, the Most Merciful.

Rahmān (A) God, the Most Compassionate.

Rasūl ☺ (A) Prophet Muhammad ☺, the Messenger of Allāh.

rasi (T) A sign of the zodiac.

rūh (A) The soul, the Light ray of God, the Light of God's wisdom. Bawa Muhaiyaddeen ☺ explains that the *rūh* is life, *hayāt*. Out of the six kinds of lives, the soul is the Light life, the human life. It is a ray of the *Nūr*, Light of Allāh, a ray that does not die or disappear. It comes from Allāh and returns to Allāh.

S

sabūr (A) Patience; inner patience; to go within patience, to accept it, to think and reflect within it. *Sabūr* is that patience deep within patience which comforts, soothes, and alleviates mental suffering. Literally, *sabūr* is the intensive form of *sabr* or patience.

sannyasi (T) Renunciate, mendicant, ascetic.

sattiya vedam (T) The religion of truth.

Shaikh (A) The Guru; the teacher who takes the disciples to the shore of the heart; a spiritual teacher.

shakti (T) The energy or force of creation arising from the five elements; also refers to the consort of Sivan.

shakūr (A) Gratitude; contentment with whatever may happen, realizing that everything comes from Allāh; contentment arising from gratitude.

shari (T) All right, correct, good.

shastras (T) Horoscopes; six philosophical books in Hinduism.

siddhi (T) Occult power, miracle; the ability to perform miracles acquired by devotion to and control of the elements.

sifāt (A) Form, creation, manifestation.

Sivan and Shakti (T) Adam ☺ and Eve ☺; the section of earth, creation.

subhānallāhi kalimah (A) The *subhānallāhi kalimah* is recited to sacrifice the animal qualities in man that cause him to hurt other lives; the third of the five *kalimahs.* Also known as *tasbīh,* the third *kalimah.*

sūrat (A) Form.

suwādarnam (T) Purity, health, cleanliness.

swami, swamiar (T) Teacher, ascetic.

T

tahappan (T) Father.

tambi (T) Younger brother.

tānam, nidānam, avadānam, gnānam (T) Surrender, perfect balance, absolute focus, and divine wisdom.

tantra (T) Stratagem, scheme, trick.

tārahan, singhan, sūran (T) The three sons of illusion, related to aspects of the sexual act.

tasbīh (A) Glorification of God; the *subhānallāhi kalimah.* Literally, saying, "*Subhānallāh,* glory is God's."

tattwa (T) The strength or power that is inherent in the qualities of the creations, manifesting through the action of each respective quality; potentialities. While jinns, demons, and ghosts have thirty-six *tattwas,* man has ninety-six, and through these he can control everything.

taubah (A) Repentance; to ask forgiveness from God for sins and errors, to turn away from them, and to vow never to commit them again.

tawakkul, tawakkulun 'alAllāh (A) Absolute trust in God; surrender to God; handing over to God the entire responsibility for everything.

tiyānam (T) Meditation.

tonnūru onbathu (T) Ninety-nine.

U

unarchi (T) Awareness; the second of the seven levels of wisdom.

unarvu (T) Feeling, perception; the first of the seven levels of wisdom.

utāranam (T) Example, illustration, proof, authority.

V

vanakkam (T) Prayer, worship; also a greeting.

Varunabagavān (T) The Hindu god of water.

Vāyubagavān (T) The Hindu god of air.

veda (T) Scripture, religion.

vedanta (T) Philosophy.

velichcham (T) Resplendence.

vilinta poit (T) Absorbed and gone.

vingnānam (T) Science, scientific inquiry.

W

wahy (A) Revelation, inspiration from God; the commandments or words of God that were transmitted by Angel Gabriel ☉ to Prophet Muhammad ☺.

waqt (A) Time; one of the five times of prayer each day, in Islam. But truly, there is only one *waqt*. That is the prayer that never ends, where one is in direct communication with God and one is merged in God.

wilāyat (A) God's Power; that which manifests through God's actions; the ninety-nine beautiful names and actions of God.

Y

Yahweh (H) God, Jehovah.

yuga (T) An age; one of the four ages of the world. According to Bawa Muhaiyaddeen ☺ the world has been in existence two hundred million years and is divided into four yugas of fifty million years each.

Index

Passim denotes that the references are not to be found on all of the listed pages; e.g., 24-29 *passim* would be used where the reference is on pages 24, 25, 27, and 29. **Bold** signifies substantial references.

About Qutb
M. R. Bawa Muhaiyaddeen ⓡ

The teachings of Muhammad Raheem Bawa Muhaiyaddeen ⓡ express the mystical explanation, the SUFI path of esoteric Islam; namely that the human being is uniquely created with the faculty of Wisdom, enabling one to trace consciousness back to its origin—Allah, the one divine Being, the Creator of all—and to surrender the self within that Source, leaving the One God, the Truth, as the only reality in one's life. He spoke endlessly of this Truth through parables, discourses, songs and stories, all pointing the way to return to God.

People from all religions and races flocked to hear and be near him; he taught everyone, regardless of origin, with love, compassion and acceptance. An extraordinary being, he taught from experience, having traversed the Path, and returned, divinely aware—sent back to exhort all who yearn for the experience of God to discover this internal Wisdom, the path of surrender to that One.

M. R. Bawa Muhaiyaddeen's known history begins in Sri Lanka. He was discovered in the pilgrimage town of Kataragama by spiritual seekers from the northern city of Jaffna. Begging him to come teach them, he did so for forty years until 1971, when he accepted an American invitation to Philadelphia, from where he lovingly taught until his passing in December, 1986.

In these distressing times, his teachings are increasingly recognized as representing the original intention of Islam which is Purity—the relationship between man and God as explained by all the prophets of God, from Adam to Noah, Abraham, Moses, Jesus and Muhammad, may the peace of God be upon them—all sent to tell and retell mankind that there is one and only one God, and that this One is their source, attainable, and waiting for the return of each individual soul.

The Bawa Muhaiyaddeen Fellowship is in Philadelphia, Pennsylvania, which was the home of M. R. Bawa Muhaiyaddeen ☺ when he lived in the United States. The Fellowship continues to serve as a meeting house, as a reservoir of people and materials for everyone wishing access to his teachings.

The Mosque of Shaikh M. R. Bawa Muhaiyaddeen is located on the same property; here the five daily prayers and Friday congregational prayers are observed. An hour west of the Fellowship is the Mazār, the resting place of M. R. Bawa Muhaiyaddeen ☺ which is open daily between sunrise and sunset.

If you would like to visit the Fellowship, or to obtain a schedule of current events, branch locations and meetings, please contact:

The Bawa Muhaiyaddeen Fellowship
5820 Overbrook Avenue
Philadelphia, Pennsylvania 19131

Phone: **(215) 879-6300**
or **(215) 879-8604** (voice mail)
Fax: **(215) 879-6307**

E-mail: **info@bmf.org**
Website: **www.bmf.org**

Books in Print by
M. R. Bawa Muhaiyaddeen ﷺ

God's Psychology: A Sufi Explanation

The Point Where God and Man Meet

The Map of the Journey to God: Lessons from the School of Grace

The Golden Words of a Sufi Sheikh, Revised Edition

Islam and World Peace: Explanations of a Sufi, Revised Edition

A Book of God's Love

The Resonance of Allah: Resplendent Explanations
Arising from the *Nūr, Allāh's* Wisdom of Grace

The Tree That Fell to the West: Autobiography of a Sufi

Asmā'ul Husnā: The 99 Beautiful Names of Allah

Questions of Life—Answers of Wisdom (Vols. 1, 2)

The Fast of Ramadan: The Inner Heart Blossoms

Hajj: The Inner Pilgrimage

The Triple Flame: The Inner Secrets of Sufism

A Song of Muhammad ⊖

To Die Before Death: The Sufi Way of Life

A Mystical Journey

Sheikh and Disciple

Why Can't I See the Angels:
Children's Questions to a Sufi Saint

Treasures of the Heart: Sufi Stories for Young Children

Come to the Secret Garden: Sufi Tales of Wisdom

My Love You My Children:
101 Stories for Children of All Ages

Maya Veeram or The Forces of Illusion

God, His Prophets and His Children

Four Steps to Pure *Iman*

The Wisdom of Man

(continued on next page)

Truth & Light: Brief Explanations

Songs of God's Grace

The Guidebook to the True Secret of the Heart (Vols. 1, 2)

The Divine Luminous Wisdom That Dispels the Darkness

Wisdom of the Divine (Vols. 1–6)

The Tasty, Economical Cookbook (Vols. 1, 2)

Booklets

GEMS OF WISDOM SERIES:

Vol. 1: The Value of Good Qualities

Vol. 2: Beyond Mind and Desire

Vol. 3: The Innermost Heart

Vol. 4: Come to Prayer

Pamphlets

Advice to Prisoners

Du'ā' Kanzul-'Arsh (The Invocation of the Treasure of the Throne)

Faith

The Golden Words of a Sufi Sheikh: Preface to the Book

In Commemoration of the Sixth Anniversary of the Opening of
The Mosque of Shaikh M. R. Bawa Muhaiyaddeen ☺

Islam & World Peace: Explanations of a Sufi – Jihad, The Holy War Within

Islam & World Peace: Explanations of a Sufi – The True Meaning of Islam
and Epilogue

Islam & World Peace: Explanations of a Sufi – Two Discourses

Letter to the World Family

Love is the Remedy, God is the Healer

The Pond -- A Letter to the Fellowship Family

A Prayer for Father's Day

A Prayer for My Children

A Prayer from My Heart

Strive for a Good Life

Sufi: A Brief Explanation

A Sufi Perspective on Business
25 Duties – The True Meaning of Fellowship
With Every Breath, Say *lā Ilāha Ill-Allāhu*
Who is God?
Why Man Has No Peace (from My Love You, My Children)
Why We Recite the Maulids
The Wisdom and Grace of the Sufis

A CONTEMPORARY SUFI SPEAKS:
To Teenagers and Parents
On the Signs of Destruction
On Peace of Mind
On the True Meaning of Sufism
On Unity: The Legacy of the Prophets
The Meaning of Fellowship
Mind, Desire, and the Billboards of the World

FOREIGN LANGUAGE PUBLICATIONS

Ein Zeitgenössischer Sufi Spricht über Inneren Frieden
(A Contemporary Sufi Speaks on Peace of Mind—
German translation)

Deux Discours tirés du Livre L'Islam et la Paix Mondiale:
Explications d'un Soufi
(Two Discourses from the Book, Islam and World Peace:
Explanations of a Sufi—French translation)

¿Quién es Dios? Una Explicatión por el Sheikh Sufi
(Who is God? An Explanation by the Sufi Sheikh—
Spanish translation)

Other Publications

Bawa Muhaiyaddeen Fellowship Calendar

Inner & Universal Meanings of Islam
(An article about M. R. Bawa Muhaiyaddeen ☺ and Islam:
Reprinted from the Harvard Divinity Bulletin.)

Al-hamdu lillāh!
All praise belongs to God!
Any errors or omissions are ours.